Types of Cannon

Culvern

Cannon

Pedrero

Mortar

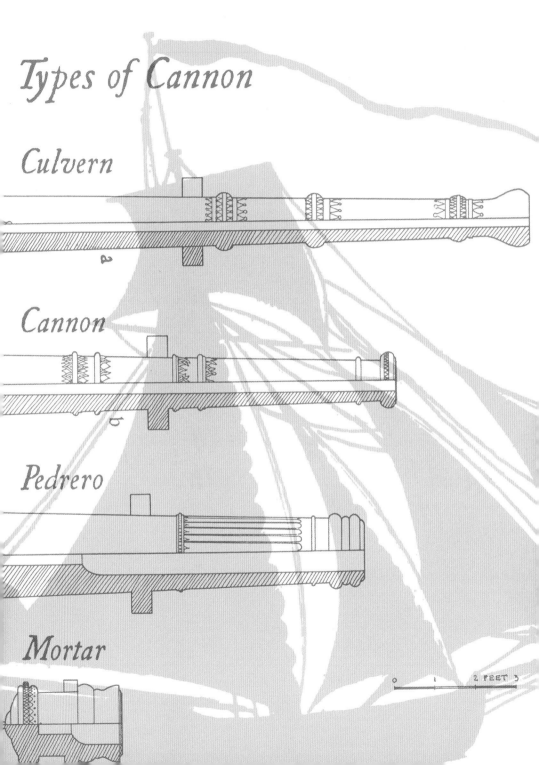

0   1   2 FEET 3

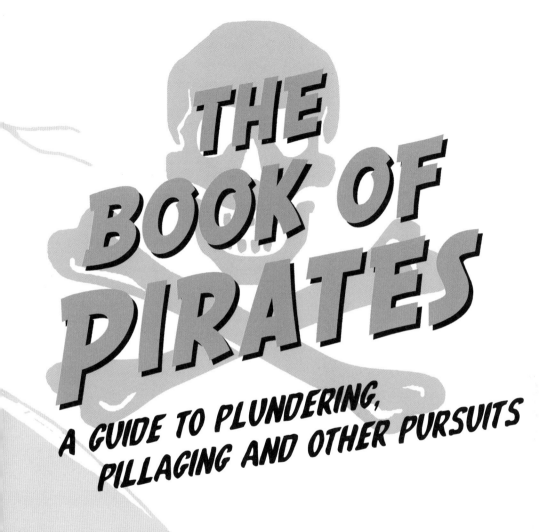

THE BOOK OF PIRATES

A GUIDE TO PLUNDERING, PILLAGING AND OTHER PURSUITS

JAMAICA ROSE & CAPTAIN MICHAEL MACLEOD

GIBBS SMITH
TO ENRICH AND INSPIRE HUMANKIND

To our own little pirates: Angela,
Brooke, Michaela, and Zoey.

To Jamaica Rose's mom: Proofreader and fact-checker.

To Cap'n Michael's father:
Thanks Dad, for inspiring in me my love of the sea.

First Edition
14 13 12 11 10   5 4 3 2

Text © 2010 Jamaica Rose and Captain Michael MacLeod
Illustrations © 2010 as noted throughout and on page 219

Published by
Gibbs Smith
P.O. Box 667
Layton, Utah 84041

1.800.835.4993 orders
www.gibbs-smith.com

Designed by Kurt Wahlner
Manufactured in China in July 2010 by Toppan.
Gibbs Smith books are printed on either recycled, 100% post-
consumer waste, FSC-certified papers or on paper produced from
a 100% certified sustainable forest/controlled wood source.

Library of Congress Cataloging-in-Publication Data

Rose, Jamaica.
    The book of pirates : a guide to plundering, pillaging, and other
pursuits / Jamaica Rose & Michael MacLeod.— 1st ed.
        p. cm.
    Includes index.
    ISBN-13: 978-1-4236-0670-3
    ISBN-10: 1-4236-0670-1
    1. Pirates. 2. Piracy. I. MacLeod, Michael, 1953- II. Title.
    G535.R67 2010
    910.4'5—dc22
                                2010009086

CONTENTS

ACKNOWLEDGMENTS

These are the people who inspired us and taught us the Way of the Pirates:

Karen Balentine (Piranha Swann Kidd); Paul Barton (Stynky Tudor—Pyracy Pub); John Baur (Ol' Chumbucket of Talk Like a Pirate Day); Richard Becker (pirate artist); Captain Erik Berliner (taught us sailing & navigation); Robert Chapin (swordmaster); Benjamin Cherry (Blackbeard—A New Spirit); Barry Clifford (Expedition Whydah); Dr. David Cordingly (Under the Black Flag); Anthony De Longis (stage combat trainer); Joseph Ditler (Joe Row, Jamaica Rose's secret tryst); Joan Druett (our favorite Kiwi Maritime Historian); Michael and KallieMarie Dugal (touchstones); Bryan Dunn (The Sage Lion); Tamara Eastman (our Anne Bonny connection); Eugene Eckert (Baron von Eisenfaust); Captain Finbar Gittelman (Schooner Wolf); Ed Foxe (Pirate Historian across the Pond); Mallory Geller & Jan McCall (Mallory & McCall); Nancy Gray (Agnes the Red, costumer extraordinaire); Kendra Guffey (PirateMaster); Dennis Hanon (Capt. Syn); Steve Harness (Greydog Blackwheel); Gary Harper (Gunner Gary); Graham Harris (Oak Island); Danny Hennigar (Oak Island); Skip Henderson (shantyman); Brant Johnson (Roger the Red); Kenneth J. Kinkor (Expedition Whydah historian); Ray Kula (Kapt. Kula); Louie Lambie (Pirate Louie); Lane Leonard (for suggesting Pop Rocks); Benerson Little (The Sea Rover's Practice); Alice Livermore (Mother Rackett); Don Maitz (pirate artist); Evaine Mansfield (Pilot of the Caribbean); Steve Mata; Dan McGrew (Duncan McGregor); Tony Malesic (Fiddler's Green); Liese Maloy (Philistina d'Morte); Julie McEnroe (Pirates in Paradise); Sam Miller (who sneaks us into Disney pirate sets); David Moore (Queen Anne's Revenge archeologist); James L. Nelson (for writing advice); Alice Palacio (Alice York Bradford); Steve and Alice Palacio (Blackmark Noriega); George Pepper (Capt. Cayenne); Gerard J. Reyes (The Spanish Pirate); Roderick the Sly (Fiddlers Green); Jon Rose (God's Own Pyrotechnician); Michael "the Tailor" Sackrison (Fiddler's Green); Capt. Horatio Sinbad (Meka II); Ernest Seliceo (Captain Jamie Bellows); Gail Selinger (Cap'n Ned, who got Jamaica Rose into the Sweet Trade); Michael Short (Tavish—Cossack Pirate); Elisabeth Shure (Dibba); Spydr; Rose Stayduhar (Rotten Rosie); John Richard Stephens (Dead Men Tell No Tales); Sgt. Charles L. Suggs, USMC Ret. (Shark); Mark Summers (Cap'n Slappy of Talk Like a Pirate Day); Mitcheal Toles (Mad Eye Mitch); Amy Weyand (Barracuda d'Morte); Arthur Whittam (Cascabel—Flintlocks 101); Jefferson Wilmore (Jules Evermore); Glenn Woodbury (Arctic explorer); Richard Zacks (The Pirate Hunter); The whole Port Royal Privateer crew; The whole Rogue Privateers crew

         . . . and lots more who we forgot to list here.

RANSOM ME THIS!

INTRO: NO PREY, NO PAY

Are you looking for adventure? Excitement? Would you like to feel the wind in your hair as you scan the horizon with your spyglass, looking for heavily laden Spanish galleons filled with treasure?

Would you like to learn how to fight with a sword or be part of a cannon crew, firing the ship's massive cast-iron guns? Or find out what those symbols on the pirate flag really mean and how to design and make your own? These are just a few of the things we've got in store for you. So, do you want to sign the articles and set sail with us?

Then come aboard! We're Jamaica Rose and Cap'n Michael—and we'll share our world of pirates with you. We'll reveal all the secrets and teach you everything you need to know to be a proper swashbuckler, buccaneer, and rogue.

Drag that rum keg over there and sit yourself down as we tell you about the pirates of old. Pirates have been sailin' the seas for more than 3,000 years now. Even the Egyptians had trouble with us.

The most famous of the rogues of the sea are the ones who sailed along the Spanish Main from the 1500s to the early 1700s. They hungered for the treasures of the New World and hunted the Spanish ships—the famed treasure galleons. They were the buccaneers and the pirates of the "Golden Age of Piracy."

Pirates are still sailin' the seas, only now they have cell phones and AK-47s instead of cutlasses and flintlocks.

Read about the wickedest pirates of all time. But learn that not all pirates were thought of as horrid criminals (at least by their own countries). Sometimes they were richly rewarded—and some were even knighted for their efforts.

This book contains everything a young buccaneer needs to advance from Landlubber to an accomplished Sea Rover. We promise you the start of the adventure of a lifetime.

The Spanish Main:

This was the coastline (areas along the coast) of the Spanish Empire that surrounded the Caribbean Sea and was the departure point for the Spanish treasure fleets.

We'll give you advice on how to:

† Make the proper costume choices to be "piratically" fashionable.
  † Find just the right pirate name.
    † Make and wield your own cutlass.
      † Get that proper fearsome look of a buccaneer, complete with a wicked scar or two.

To start off, you might be wondering who were the pirates?

Way long ago when people started traveling by water in the first boats (probably hollowed-out logs), there were other people who attacked them and stole their stuff. Those thieves were pirates. Pirates have been known by lots of names in different eras and different locations. You can learn about some of them in the next chapter. There have been river pirates, harbor pirates, and lake pirates, as well as pirates on the high seas. First and foremost, pirates are sailors. They are just a lot more CREATIVE about how they get their income.

It was not always clear exactly who was or was not a pirate. People often called their enemies pirates just to give them a bad name, even if they weren't really pirates. To this day, the British still call John Paul Jones a pirate, but he was one of the greatest American naval heroes. True pirates will rob anyone and don't care what country their victims come from. They don't get any pay unless they capture someone else's cargo or treasure, hence the saying "no prey, no pay."

WHAT IS PIRACY?

aw books will tell you the definition of piracy is "taking a ship on the High Seas." The High Seas are the parts of the ocean that are at least three miles away from a coastline. That part of the ocean doesn't belong to any country. The waters less than three miles away belong to that coastline's country. But if somebody . . .

✝ captures or attacks someone else's boat, ship, or other vessel floating on any kind of water (whether high seas, low seas, shoreline, river, or lake);
✝ fires upon the shoreline from a vessel to the shore;
✝ or uses ships to bring marauders to a shore to raid and plunder,

. . . then most people would probably call that piracy.

In fact, people like using the words "piracy" and "pirates" so much that today there is also "software piracy," "pirated music," "pirate radio," "corporate pirates," and much more. None of these have much of anything to do with water, ships, or real pirates.

So let's get back to what's really important—turning you into a proper pirate. Continue on to the next chapter and we'll look at what you think you already know about pirates.

Jamaica Rose

Michael MacLeod

Jamaica Rose and Cap'n Michael MacLeod.
Portrait by Don Maitz.

POLLY WANT A PIRATE!

PIRATE FACTS AND FICTION

Pirates! The very word conjures up all sorts of visions of swashbuckling adventures, epic sea battles, and chests full of treasure. I bet you think you know a lot about pirates. You've got some ideas about what they wore, how they lived, what sort of ships they sailed, and who was in command. Classic tales in books and movies have helped shape our thoughts about the average pirate. But how much of what you know is TRUE?

Cap'n Michael says:

Let's take a little quiz, me bucco, and see what ya really know!

Here's a Pirate's Dozen (thirteen, that is) of things people believe about pirates. Read the statements that follow and decide if you think they are true or false. Once yer done with that, finish reading this chapter ta see how many ya got right.

ONE: Pirates sank a lot of ships.
TWO: Pirates made prisoners walk the plank.
THREE: Missing body parts were a unique pirate thing.
FOUR: Most pirates wore great big boots.
FIVE: Tattoos were common among pirates.
SIX: Pirates were always drunk.
SEVEN: All pirates say "Aarrrrrh" and "Yo ho ho."
EIGHT: Pirate captains could do anything they wanted. They kept the lion's share of the treasure, and ruled their ships any way they wanted.
NINE: A lot of pirates wore gold hoop earrings.
TEN: Pirates always flew a black Jolly Roger flag, and it was a threat of DEATH.
ELEVEN: Pirates were mostly white guys from England.
TWELVE: Pirates had parrots, monkeys, and other animals as pets.
THIRTEEN: Pirate ships were huge, powerful ships with cannons everywhere.

PIRATES SANK A LOT OF SHIPS—
FALSE!

Aye, you've seen it many a time. A pirate vessel suddenly appears out of the mist, with cannons blazing, blowing holes in everything in sight. Sorry, mate, but it just ain't so. Pirates didn't want to blow holes in other ships, and they certainly DID NOT want to sink them—they wanted to PLUNDER them. It's hard to plunder a ship that has sunk to the bottom of the sea.

PIRATE TIMELINE

1176 BCE
Pharaoh Ramses III defeats the Sea Peoples (early pirates) in a great battle at the mouth of the Nile Delta.

75 BCE
Julius Caesar is kidnapped by Cilician pirates and held captive.

Instead of blowing big holes in the sides of a ship, a pirate would try to disable it by destroying the rigging (the sails and spars, and the lines holding them). When the rigging is mangled and broken, the ship cannot be controlled. Then it is much easier for the pirate to overtake and board her.

Pirates used special types of cannonballs that messed up the rigging. One type of cannonball, called a chain shot or bar shot, had two halves that separated and spread apart. Between the two halves was a chain or bar inside a bar that slid out. This type of cannonball spun around and around, doing a LOT of damage to the rigging. It made a noise like a high-pitched scream as it traveled through the air. Not only did the noise terrify people, it also acted like a gigantic saw. ANYTHING that got in its way would be torn to pieces. Seeing one of these in action might make a merchant ship's crew think seriously about surrender.

PIRATES MADE PRISONERS WALK THE PLANK – MOSTLY FALSE!

All the best pirate stories have someone walking a plank. Captain Hook made Wendy walk the plank. Captain Barbossa forced Captain Jack Sparrow and Elizabeth Swann off the *Black Pearl* via a plank.

Actually, forcing prisoners to walk a plank seems to have come along late in the pirate game. No one knows for sure where this idea came from. The first plank walking known took place in 1769. A mutineer named

0 CE   1000   1400

793 CE	1217	1401	1492	1494
Viking pirates make their first raid in England.	Medieval pirate Eustace the Monk is captured in the English Channel and executed.	North Sea pirate Klaus Störtebeker is captured and beheaded.	Christopher Columbus's first voyage to the New World.	Treaty of Tordesillas. The pope declares that the New World belongs to Spain and Portugal.

Walking the Plank
by Howard Pyle

George Wood confessed that his crew had made prisoners walk the plank. These were not pirates, though many mutineers did become pirates.

It was not until 1822 that pirates made prisoners walk the plank. William Smith, captain of the *Blessing*, was forced to walk the plank by the pirate crew of the *Emanuel*. Some stories claim Stede Bonnet, the pirate who sailed with Blackbeard, made prisoners walk the plank, but there are no records of this. Most victims were just killed and thrown over the side.

MISSING BODY PARTS WERE A UNIQUE PIRATE THING— FALSE!

Look at just about any cartoon of a pirate, and he either has a hook instead of a hand, or a peg leg instead of a foot, or a patch covering up a missing eye—or maybe all three.

True, being a pirate was a hazardous life, and pirates got injured—a LOT. The pirate articles (rules pirates agreed to) had orders giving extra shares of the treasure to pirates who lost limbs or eyes. They got even more if they lost their right arm instead of their left (because most pirates were right-handed). Whether the injured pirate could still be a useful part of the crew was another question.

Articles:
Rules the pirate crew voted on and agreed to live by.

But were pirates the only ones who lost body parts? Were eye patches, hooks, and peg legs uniquely piratical accessories?

EYE PATCH

If you see someone with an eye patch, you immediately think "pirate." It is easy to imagine a pirate losing an eye in a sea battle or a sword

An old sailor with TWO peg legs and an eye patch

1500

Cap'n Michael says:

fight. The earliest reliable record of a one-eyed pirate with an eye patch we can find is that of Rahmah ibn Jabir al-Jalahimah (an Arab pirate), who died in 1826. There might have been others, but no one wrote about them, so we just don't know.

Some people think pirates might have worn eye patches to help their vision adjust quickly from the bright sunlight on deck to the dark underbelly of the ship. The TV show *MythBusters* tested this out, and it does seem to be a pretty good idea.

Out in the bright sunlight, the eye patch is worn over one eye to keep it used to the dark. When a pirate (or sailor) had to run belowdecks, he could switch the patch to the other eye, and he could instantly see in the dim light. He didn't have to wait for his eyes to adjust. But if this did happen, no one wrote about it.

There were (and still are) lots of non-piratical people with only one eye.

The British admiral Horatio Nelson was blind in one eye. However, he did NOT wear an eye patch (even though some paintings and statues show him with one).

The famous Spanish admiral Don Blas de Lezo also lost an eye, and he did not wear an eye patch either.

Around 1545, the young Spanish princess Ana de Mendoza y la Cerda was horsing around with one of the royal guards when the tip of his rapier accidentally poked out her eye. She did not let this stop her. In fact, she turned it to her advantage. Despite missing an eye, as Princess Ana grew up in the royal court, she became known as a great beauty. The eye patch just added to her mystique. Every dress she owned had a matching bejeweled eye patch.

So, when your mom says, "Be careful, you'll poke your eye out," you might want to listen to her. It could happen.

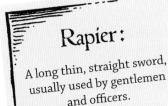

Rapier:

A long thin, straight sword, usually used by gentlemen and officers.

1550

1523	1546	1562–69	1573	1588
Jean Fleury seizes three galleons filled with silver, bound for Spain.	**Khizr Barbarossa** dies after a long, successful career as a Barbary corsair.	**John Hawkins** raids the Spanish Main.	**Francis Drake** captures a Spanish silver shipment crossing the Isthmus of Panama.	**The Spanish Armada** is defeated by the English.

HOOK

Many sailors and pirates were injured in sea battles and sailing accidents. Cannonballs whizzing across from the enemy ship did a lot of damage. Flying ropes and pullies from broken rigging whipping around could easily shatter someone's bones. Surgeons were still learning a lot about dealing with injuries and infections. Back then, usually the best they could do was to hack off the injured limb. Despite all those amputations, no real pirates are known to have worn hooks. Although it would help explain a lot of the missing eyes . . .

Pirate captain William Condon had a shooting battle with a mutineer. Condon killed the mutineer, but not before the mutineer shot Condon in the arm and shattered the bones. The arm had to be amputated. The Barbary pirate Aruj Barbarossa lost an arm in battle with a Spanish enemy. Both Admiral Horatio Nelson and Admiral Don Blas de Lezo, whom we met above, were each missing an arm. There is no record of any of these men having hooks.

The idea of a pirate with a hook seems to have started with Captain Hook in *Peter Pan*, though there were plenty of sailors who had hooks.

PEG LEG

Unlike eye patches and hooks, we do know about some pirates with wooden legs. There were two well-known pirate captains with peg legs.

The first was the Frenchman Francois LeClerc, whose nicknames were Pata de Palo ("wooden leg" in Spanish) and Jambe de Bois (French for "wooden leg"). He was not exactly a pirate. He was a French privateer (sort of a legal pirate . . . we explain on page 56). Despite having a peg leg (and a severely damaged hand, but no hook), he was quite an active pirate. He liked to hunt for Spanish treasure galleons and burn villages along the Spanish Main. He died in 1563.

The second known pirate captain with a wooden leg was the Dutch pirate Cornelis Jol. He was also called Pata de Palo, or Houtebeen (Dutch for "wooden leg"). Before he became a pirate, he was an admiral in the Dutch West India Company. Like LeClerc, he was also more privateer than pirate, and he too liked to hunt treasure-filled Spanish galleons. He never captured one, but he did attack many Spanish towns and ships. He died in 1641.

There are many accounts of peg-legged sailors who became cooks. It was a job they could do and still be at sea. With only one leg, it's very hard and dangerous to climb the

1600

1593	1600–43	1608–09	1612
Irish female pirate Grania ny Mhaille (Grace O'Malley) meets with Queen Elizabeth I.	Dutch corsairs (*pechelingues*) raid the Spanish colonies in the West Indies.	Sir Thomas Verney leaves England and his inheritance, and turns corsair.	Pirate hunter Sir Henry Mainwaring turns pirate himself and joins the corsairs.

rigging. Long John Silver in *Treasure Island* made the image of the one-legged pirate cook famous.

MOST PIRATES WORE GREAT BIG BOOTS— PROBABLY FALSE!

To be a pirate, you've got to have those big up-to-the-knee boots with the wide folded-over cuffs, what they called bucket-top boots. Right?

Actually, if you look at the various pictures of pirate captains from the 1600s and 1700s—pictures that were drawn in the 1600s and 1700s—the captains are all wearing *shoes*, not boots. Boots were not practical onboard ship. They would be hard to move about in, hard to climb the rigging in, and next to impossible to kick off if you fell overboard. On ship, sailors often went barefoot. It was easier for climbing the rigging.

But those big boots *were* useful on land for going through the jungles and brush. Even so, most drawings of Henry Morgan and other buccaneers attacking Spanish towns show them wearing shoes. There are several drawings of buccaneers who lived off the land. They are shown wearing moccasin-like shoes or are barefoot with leather hides wrapped around their legs.

TATTOOS WERE COMMON AMONG PIRATES— MOSTLY FALSE!

Tattooing is an old art. Many ancient tribes used tattoos. However, the word "tattoo" was not used

Captain Edward England wearing shoes

1616	1628	1642	1649
Mainwaring returns to England, is pardoned, and writes a treatise on piracy.	Piet Heyn, in charge of a Dutch fleet, captures a complete Spanish treasure fleet.	Tortuga is taken over by French *boucaniers*.	The English Civil War: The English decide they don't need a king. King Charles I is beheaded. England is ruled by a Commonwealth. Many of King Charles' supporters flee to the New World. Some become pirates.

by Europeans until 1769. When Captain James Cook made his famous visits to the various Polynesian islands, the sailors saw the natives with tattooing all over their bodies. Many of the sailors got tattoos from the natives as a souvenir of visiting the South Pacific. It became quite fashionable.

Sailors with large tattoos of a sailing ship on their chest or a mermaid on their biceps did not become popular until after Captain Cook's voyages.

But, long before Captain Cook visited Polynesia, William Dampier, a buccaneer and pirate himself, told how sailors used tattooing. He wrote: "the Jerusalem Cross is made in men's arms, by pricking the skin, and rubbing in a pigment . . .

Jerusalem Cross

(gun) powder." The sailors pricked their skin with a sharp needle and some gunpowder to make a small design of a cross.

So, before the 1800s, a sailor (and pirate) might have a small design of a stylized cross as a tattoo, but not until later did the large, complex tattoos show up.

PIRATES WERE ALWAYS DRUNK – MOSTLY TRUE!

Stories tell of how pirates drank rum all the time, and if they ran out of rum, they complained about it.

Yes, pirates did complain when the rum ran out. Blackbeard was involved in just such a dicey occasion. He wrote about it in his journal: "Rum all out . . . rogues a-plotting." The crew was getting ugly, and things might have gone badly; but in the nick of time, they captured a ship that had a cargo of spirits aboard. Blackbeard's crewmen were happy again, and drunk, and the problems were avoided for awhile.

Onboard ship, you might easily run out of fresh water. It often spoiled, turning slimy and green. Drinking alcohol (beer, wine, rum, brandy, etc.) was much safer than drinking water. Bacteria does not live in alcohol, so while getting drunk was not all that good for you, it was much better than dying from disease. AND a lot more fun.

1650

1655
Jamaica is captured by the English.

1660
The Restoration: The English decide they need a king after all. Charles II (son of the beheaded Charles I) is crowned. Many supporters of the Commonwealth flee to the New World. Some become pirates.

1660
The English port on Jamaica is renamed "Port Royal" in honor of the king being restored to the throne.

ALL PIRATES SAY "AARRRRRH" AND "YO HO HO" – FALSE!

Pirates had a special way of talking. There is even now a special day to celebrate this—"Talk Like a Pirate Day" on September 19. But how did pirates talk? Did they talk like the pirates in movies? Like Long John Silver? Did they say "Aarrrrrh" all the time, peppered in between with "Yo ho ho"?

We can blame the actor who played Long John Silver in the classic *Treasure Island* (1950) for this one. His name was Robert Newton, and he was British. He had a natural accent that used the "Aaaarrrh" sound. People loved his Long John Silver character, and the movie was VERY popular. So afterwards, everybody thought pirates sounded like him. Just like the past few years—after *Pirates of the Caribbean* came out—everyone thought pirates talked and acted like Captain Jack Sparrow.

But pirates came from all over and had many different accents. There were pirates with Irish accents, Scottish accents, French accents, Spanish accents, Welsh accents, Cockney accents, etc., even in the same crew. In fact, they spoke many different languages. So maybe a few sounded like Robert Newton, but not many.

CAPTAINS COULD DO ANYTHING THEY WANTED. THEY KEPT THE LION'S SHARE OF THE TREASURE AND RULED THEIR SHIPS ANY WAY THEY WANTED – FALSE!

Pirates elected their captains. If they didn't like how he was running things, they could "unelect" him and vote in a new captain. The whole crew made major decisions by group vote.

There was also another officer who was about as powerful as a captain, if not more so. That was the quartermaster. The crew elected him, too. The captain was in charge during battles, but at other times, the quartermaster usually ran things.

As for dividing up plunder and treasure, there were strict rules about this, which the whole pirate crew agreed to. These were called the *articles*. According to the ship's articles, the captain was usually given two shares, while crewmen got one share. Thus, a captain got twice as much treasure as the rest of the crew, but they did not get huge piles of treasure that they hid away in treasure caves or buried in the sand.

1662	1667–1669	1670	1671	1675
Port Royal invites buccaneers from Tortuga to use their port as home base.	**Henry Morgan's buccaneers sack Maracaibo, Portobelo, and Cuba.**	**Roche Braziliano terrorizes the Spanish.**	**The sack of Panama by Henry Morgan's buccaneers.**	**Sir Henry Morgan becomes lieutenant governor of Jamaica and suppresses piracy.**

A LOT OF PIRATES WORE GOLD HOOP EARRINGS – MAYBE SOME. BUT WE'RE NOT SURE!

Pirates are often shown wearing gold hoop earrings. However, in the accounts written by pirates and the people who met pirates, there seems to be no mention of pirates wearing earrings. Earrings are not even mentioned in the pirate classics *Treasure Island* or *Peter Pan*.

There is a pirate flag design that shows a skull in profile, wearing a bandanna and earring, but that flag design has been shown to be a fairly modern design.

There was a pirate by name of Theophilus Turner (no relation to Will Turner). He was a member of Robert Culliford's pirate crew and also sailed with Captain William Kidd. There is a listing of things taken from him when he was arrested. In the list of items were two gold earrings. The thing is, we don't know if Theo WORE the earrings or just had them because they were part of his share of the loot.

A painting of a pirate by Howard Pyle seems to be the first illustration to show hoop earrings. Douglas Fairbanks Sr. was the first pirate to wear hoop earrings in the movies, seen in *The Black Pirate*.

So why is the idea of pirates wearing earrings so common? There is a common superstition (backed up a little by acupuncture beliefs) that if you pierce an ear, you will improve the eyesight of the eye on the opposite side. Musketmen and snipers would be very interested in this.

Some believe (even now) that piercing your ear improves night vision, prevents seasickness, and provides protection against drowning or going down with the ship.

And if you did drown and washed ashore somewhere, the people who found you were supposed to pay for your burial with the gold earring. Some sailors put the name of their home port on the inside of the earring. This way the body could be sent home to the dead pirate's family for burial.

Also, even now, many sailors get their ear pierced as a badge of honor. They do this for perhaps having gone round the Horn (the southern tip of South America) or crossing the equator.

1700

1692	1692	1695	1697–99	1701
A powerful earthquake sinks two-thirds of Port Royal, Jamaica.	Thomas Tew captures a tribute ship of the Grand Moghul.	Captain John Every (Avery) captures the Grand Moghul's ship.	William Kidd is sent to hunt pirates but turns pirate himself.	William Kidd is hanged after being tried for piracy and murder.

PIRATES ALWAYS FLEW A BLACK JOLLY ROGER FLAG, AND IT WAS A THREAT OF DEATH—
FALSE!

The black pirate flag struck fear in the hearts of those who saw it on a ship coming toward them. They knew it meant PIRATES! And those pirates were going to kill them all! All pirates flew a black Jolly Roger flag with some type of skull and crossbones design on it. You just wouldn't be a pirate without it, right?

Jolly Roger:
A popular name for the black flag with skull and crossbones flown by pirates.

The first black flag was not seen until the year 1700. Before that, pirates flew a red flag. This was the Bloody Flag and meant "No Quarter Given." To "give quarter" meant to show mercy. So this red flag meant "no mercy shown . . . we will kill you all."

The black flag actually meant, "If you do not fight against us, we will not hurt you." Pirates

learned it was good for the business to advertise. They wanted to encourage the sailors on the other ship to let them take the cargo without fighting back. Fighting was messy and a lot of hard work. And you could possibly get KILLED. So, pirates preferred not to do it. But, if anyone fought back, then down came the black flag, and up went the red one (and sometimes they flew both at the same time, probably because they didn't have time to take down the black one).

1717
The pirate ship *Whydah* is wrecked off the coast of Cape Cod.

1718
As governor, former privateer Woodes Rogers expels pirates from New Providence in the Bahamas.

1718
Blackbeard is killed in battle at Ocracoke Inlet, North Carolina.

1720
The famous female pirates Anne Bonny and Mary Read are captured.

PIRATES WERE MOSTLY WHITE GUYS FROM ENGLAND – FALSE!

Actually, recent studies have shown that about one-third of the pirates were of African descent or of mixed race. Some pirate crews (though not all) treated other races as equals. It varied from crew to crew, but these men found themselves much more welcome among pirate crews than among society in general at that time.

Many were escaped or freed slaves with a grudge against those who enslaved them. Most of them would fight

Many pirates we know about were teenagers.

to the death rather than be taken prisoner and become a slave again. Many of them had reputations as fierce warriors. This would have made them very attractive to the pirates as crewmen.

There were also Hispanic pirates, Asian pirates—pirates of all races and types. They were from many different countries, yet they worked together for a common goal.

And they weren't all men. Many pirates were women. They weren't all grown-ups either. There are many pirates we know about who were teenagers or even younger.

1750   1800

1720–22
Bartholomew Roberts threatens the Guinea Coast and West Indies.

1776–80
More than two thousand American privateers aid the American Revolution and harass British shipping.

1804
In the First Barbary War, Stephen Decatur blows up the captured American ship *Philadelphia* so the Barbary corsairs could not use her.

A Spanish hidalgo *(soldier of fortune) followed by his slave carrying a tamed parrot.*

1805
 A handful of U.S. Marines capture Derna, Tripoli (part of modern-day Libya) from Barbary pirates. This event is honored by the line "To the shores of Tripoli" in the "U.S. Marines' Hymn."

1807
 Chinese pirate chief Zheng Yi dies. His wife Ching Shih takes over as leader and becomes even more powerful. Soon she is leader of the largest fleet of pirate ships ever assembled.

1810
 Ching Shih accepts an offer of amnesty from the Chinese government. She keeps her loot and opens a gambling house.

PIRATES HAD PARROTS, MONKEYS, AND OTHER ANIMALS AS PETS—
POSSIBLY TRUE!

Long John Silver had a parrot. Barbossa had a monkey. Didn't every captain have some sort of pet?

The exotic birds of the Americas, and especially the talking parrots and mynahs, had been a big hit back in London. If a sailor brought back a parrot, he could sell it. On the long voyage home, if he had trained it to do some tricks or say some words, he could sell it for quite a bit, and with the meager income sailors received, this would be a nice bonus. Sailors also brought monkeys, iguanas, and other exotic creatures back home to sell or give to their wives or children. In the late 1600s, William Dampier, sailing with a band of buccaneers, wrote: "Here are also kept tame Monkeys, Parrots, Parakites, &c, which the Seamen carry home."

We know that sailors and sometimes bands of buccaneers brought birds and other exotic animals aboard ship. But it's not clear if any of them kept the animals after returning to port and having a chance to sell them.

PIRATE SHIPS WERE HUGE, POWERFUL SHIPS WITH CANNONS EVERYWHERE—
MOSTLY FALSE!

You've probably seen the pirate movies where two big ships come barreling at each other with their guns thundering. A big bad pirate had a big bad pirate ship—a huge sailing beast just bristling with cannons everywhere—just the thing for robbing and plundering people, no?

Actually, pirates often hugged the coastlines and shallow waters. They waited to pounce on passing ships and wanted to hide from the big naval vessels on patrol. Pirates would much rather run away than fight with another big ship. Maybe that doesn't sound very brave, but they weren't interested in fighting if they didn't have to. They were all about the plunder. Naval vessels usually had no treasure worth stealing.

1850

1815	1815	1818	1832–1865
Pirates Jean and Pierre Lafitte assist Andrew Jackson in the Battle of New Orleans.	The Second Barbary War: Stephen Decatur "persuades" the Dey of Algiers to sign a peace treaty.	Hippolyte de Bouchard attacks the coast of California.	England establishes the Far Eastern Command of the British Navy to suppress piracy in the South China Sea and Southeast Asia.

For a pirate, speed was a much more important quality than power, along with the ability to go into shallow waters, where they could thumb their noses at the big powerful warship that couldn't catch them (as long as they were out of cannon range).

Some pirates did have big ships, such as Blackbeard and Bartholomew Roberts. But they also had several smaller vessels sailing along with it as consorts (escort vessels). The big ship was the flagship: powerful and intimidating but not very quick and agile. The smaller vessels were the quick ones that could overtake a prey or cut off any escape route by working in pairs.

Do not underestimate the abilities of a handful of pirates in a small open boat. There were several times when such a band of desperate men successfully took on and captured much larger craft.

1900

1861–1865
  During the American Civil War, the Confederacy commissions privateers to battle Union naval forces. The U.S. refuses to recognize the Confederate Navy ships and considers them pirates. Confederate blockade runners that smuggled goods into the South are also sometimes considered pirates.

1920s–1930s
  In China, civil war and widespread corruption creates an ideal breeding ground for pirates in the South China Sea. Pirates operate out of most of the ports and waterways in the region.

2009
  Four Somalian pirates seize the *Maersk Alabama* and hold the captain hostage until rescued by U.S. Navy SEALs.

PIRATES OF THE CARIBBEAN

The dots on a map that represent the Caribbean Islands look like pearls strung on a necklace. They start along the Venezuelan coast, first heading east. The necklace curves north and then west. The islands get larger and larger as they head toward the tip of Florida, ending in the largest of them all, Cuba. All together, they are called the Caribbean Islands. They curl around the Caribbean Sea on the east and north. On the west is Central America. To the south are the countries of Colombia and Venezuela.

Together the four largest islands—Cuba, Jamaica, Hispaniola (which is now split into two countries: Haiti and the Dominican Republic), and Puerto Rico—are the "Greater Antilles." So guess what the rest of the islands are called? You've got it—the "Lesser Antilles." The Lesser Antilles were also called the Caribbee Islands, named for the Carib Indians who lived there (a fierce, cannibalistic tribe).

Where did the name "Antilles" come from? Antilia was a mysterious land shown floating out in the ocean on some old maps, long before Columbus made his voyages. After Columbus found the islands in the New World, they were named for this mythical land.

Together, the Caribbean Islands (Greater and Lesser Antilles) combined with the Bahamas (north of Cuba) are called the West Indies. This is because Columbus was confused. He was looking for a new way to Asia. When he arrived in the Bahamas, he thought he had come to the Spice Islands of the Indies (near Indonesia) from the other way around the world. Once people realized Columbus made a mistake, they called these new islands the West Indies, and the original Indies became known as the East Indies.

SEA DOGS PUT THE BITE ON THE SPANISH

As soon as Europeans discovered the New World with Columbus's voyage of 1492, a whole new "playground" opened up, and pirates were soon there.

Spain and Portugal divvied up the New World as their own territory and tried to keep all the other European nations out. They even got the Pope to declare this in the Treaty of Tordesillas in 1494. The treaty gave most of the New World to Spain. Portugal got the area that is now Brazil. This is why Brazilians now speak Portuguese, while most other South and Central Americans speak Spanish.

SURE, WE STOLE IT, BUT THAT DOESN'T MEAN YOU CAN STEAL IT FROM US

Spanish treasure ships were bringing a vast wealth of silver, gold, and jewels back to Spain. This wealth was stolen plunder from the Aztecs in Mexico, the Incas in Peru, and other natives in the New World. The natives did not use gold and silver as money, but made beautiful jewelry and artwork out of the precious metals. The Spanish did not care about the beauty of the artwork. They melted the gold and silver down into bars, bricks, and coins. In 1521, the first Spanish Treasure Fleet sailed to Spain. The Spanish had learned it was better if several ships sailed together for protection and safety. This was because the other European countries wanted a piece of the New World pie. They had sent their pirates and privateers to grab what they could of the New World's treasures.

The French were the first to intercept the treasure galleons. In fact, it was in 1521 when French privateers captured two Spanish ships returning to Spain filled with treasure. Right away, the king of Spain sent a small fleet to rescue his ships. After a brief battle at sea, the French privateers got away but had to leave the Spanish treasure ships behind. They may have been unsuccessful, but they had seen the treasure with their own eyes, and word spread fast. Soon many other Frenchmen were trying to capture Spanish treasure ships.

A few years later, in 1523, the Frenchman Jean Fleury cruised the waters of the Atlantic Ocean between the Canary Islands and the Azores (off the west coast of northern Africa and Spain). He was hoping to head off a returning treasure ship just before it got back to Spain. Luck was with him! He captured two such ships loaded with fabulous wealth. The treasure included "gold and silver jewelry, pearls the size of filberts, jade figures, ceremonial costumes, feathered headdresses, mosaic masks, even three live jaguars."

WE ARE GOING TO TRADE, WHETHER YOU LIKE IT OR NOT

The English privateers, called Sea Dogs, joined the French in the quest for New World treasure. John Hawkins made three voyages to Spanish America starting in 1562. He first stopped in West Africa to fill his ship with African slaves. He kidnapped about four hundred Africans and forced them aboard his ship. Then he sold them at a handsome profit to Spanish plantation owners in Hispaniola, trading them for pearls, ginger, sugar, and hides. The plantation owners were eager to buy, even though Spanish laws had forbidden trading with non-Spanish traders.

After his first success, everyone wanted to invest in Hawkins' second voyage—even Queen Elizabeth I. Stopping again in West Africa, he filled his ship with another four hundred slaves. This time, the Spanish ports in the New World were closed to him since people got in trouble for trading with Hawkins the first time. However, with a little forceful arm-twisting, plus his charm, Hawkins was able to sell all his slaves again.

On his third trip to sell slaves, a storm forced him to take shelter in Veracruz. He captured the island fort of San Juan de Ulua to use as a base while he made repairs. The very next day, the Spanish Treasure Fleet showed up! He was trapped and outnumbered. The Spanish attacked. Only two of Hawkins' ships escaped: his own and the one commanded by his cousin Francis Drake. Hawkins' ship, the *Minion*, barely limped home to England. He only had fifteen men left when he arrived. Drake arrived home with few problems but vowed revenge on the Spanish for killing so many Englishmen.

A PIRATE QUEEN AND HER DRAGON

Drake was a man of his word. He soon began a series of destructive raids on several Spanish colonies. He ignored the fact that Spain and England were officially at peace. All he cared about was his driving need for revenge and treasure. His attacks during peacetime meant he was no longer a privateer—he was a PIRATE.

Soon, the Spanish just called him "El Draque." It was a play on his last name. It meant "the Dragon." He lived up to this name. Years after his death, naughty Spanish children were threatened with a visit from "El Draque," just as children now fear the bogeyman.

Name: Sir Francis Drake

Alias: El Draque (The Dragon)

Dates: 1540–1596

Country: England

Ship: *Golden Hind*

Flag: The flag of England

Best known for: Circumnavigating the earth in the *Golden Hind*, claiming the west coast of North America for England and naming it Nova Albion, and defeating the Spanish Armada.

From 1577 to 1580, Drake sailed around the world in his famous ship, the *Golden Hind*. Along the way, he plundered Spanish colonies and captured a very wealthy Spanish galleon off the Pacific Coast of South America. When he returned to England with his plundered wealth, Queen Elizabeth granted him a private audience for over six hours to listen to all of his adventures. He gave her a large portion of the stolen riches, and she fondly called him "her pirate." Soon after, in a ceremony aboard the *Golden Hind*, Drake was knighted. After this, Queen Elizabeth was called "The Pirate Queen."

THIS MEANS WAR!

Spain was furious and soon declared war on England. This eventually led to the attack of the Spanish Armada in 1588. Both Drake and Hawkins helped defend their country, along with many other Sea Dogs. Through a combination of bravery and cleverness on the part of the English, and bad luck and bad weather for the Spanish, the Armada was defeated. Hawkins was knighted for his actions during the invasion of the Spanish Armada.

English privateer John Oxenham, who accompanied Francis Drake on his sack of Panama.

For another fifteen years, Elizabeth's Sea Dogs continued to raid Spanish colonies and ships. They also explored new territories and tried to set up new English colonies in the New World. (For more on the Sea Dogs, see page 56.)

Upon the death of Queen Elizabeth I in 1603, James I of Scotland became king. He disbanded much of the navy that Elizabeth had built up. Many of the privateers and sailors were put out of work and had little hope of getting jobs on shore since they had few other skills. Starving, several of them found a solution by joining the Barbary corsairs and becoming pirates. (For more on the corsairs, see page 54.)

THE SEA BEGGARS MAKE BEGGARS OF THE SPANISH

In the late 1500s and early 1600s, the Dutch were fighting for their independence from the Spanish. The Dutch forces that fought at sea were called the Sea Beggars. At first they fought mainly in the English Channel, but the Sea Beggars soon carried the war against the Spanish to the New World. (For more on the Sea Beggars' activities in Europe, see page 56.)

In 1624, Pieter Schouten, with a small fleet of three ships, ransacked Spanish colonies on the Yucatan Peninsula (a part of present-day Mexico). A few months later, he captured one of the rich Spanish galleons from the Honduras Treasure Fleet. Towing his rich prize back to Europe, his own ship ran aground in the Dry Tortugas. He abandoned his own ship, and he and his crew sailed home aboard the Spanish galleon. The rich cargo he brought back convinced other Dutch privateers to try their luck against the Spanish in the Caribbean.

A few years later, Piet Heyn followed Schouten's example. He would be very glad he did. Heyn had little love for the Spanish. Early in his privateer career, the Spanish had captured him, chained him to an oar, and forced him to row as a galley slave.

Being a galley slave was brutal backbreaking labor. Men generally didn't survive it for very long. Somehow, Heyn managed to survive for more than four years before he was finally released in a prisoner exchange.

Piet Heyn may have started as a common sailor, but he was smart, he was ambitious, and he had developed a burning hatred of the Spanish. Piet Heyn would have his revenge. The Spanish would soon regret letting him go.

In 1628, Heyn had worked his way up to the rank of admiral. He was put in charge of a huge fleet of 31 ships and 3,300 men. This Dutch fleet set out for the Caribbean, eagerly looking to capture Spanish treasure ships.

Their plans were almost spoiled. A Dutch cabin boy got lost while ashore on an island near Venezuela. The Spanish captured him and got him to tell about the Dutch fleet lying in wait for them. So warned, the Venezuelan Treasure Fleet did not leave port.

However, the treasure fleet from Veracruz, Mexico, did not know about the Dutch waiting to ambush them. The treasure-filled galleons arrived at Havana, Cuba, only to find Heyn's ships waiting for them. Entrance to the harbor was blocked! The Spanish commander Juan de Benavides panicked.

Not knowing what to do, Benavides ran his ships aground without firing a shot at the Dutch. He was hoping to unload the silver and take it inland to safety, but the Dutch caught up with them too quickly.

It turns out that Benavides was not much of a seaman. He had gotten his job mostly because his sister

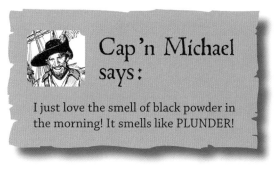

Cap'n Michael says:

I just love the smell of black powder in the morning! It smells like PLUNDER!

was one of the Spanish king's girlfriends. Up till now, he had gained a lot of wealth by smuggling illegal goods on his ships. Oh, by the way, he had been the captain of one of the ships where Heyn had been a galley slave.

Benavides later claimed he tried to attack the Dutch. However, when the Dutch captured the grounded ships and came aboard, they found so much silver and gold aboard that many of the gun ports were blocked. Heyn had captured the entire Mexican Treasure Fleet unchallenged! It included NINETY TONS of silver and gold!

On the way back to Europe, two of the captured Spanish vessels sank in a storm with some of the treasure aboard. Despite the loss of the two vessels and their treasure, and despite having so many men in the Dutch fleet, there was plenty of loot to share around and still leave a profit of more than seven million guilders for the Dutch West India Company. Some estimate the treasure Heyn captured was worth more than $15 million! Piet Heyn was a national hero. On the other hand, the Spanish commander Benavides was beheaded for having lost so much treasure and bringing such shame to Spain.

JUST A BUNCH OF JERKY MAKERS

T hroughout the 1500s, the pirates and privateers who raided the New World came from the Old World, or Europe. During the next century, that was to change. Over time, many of the pirates and privateers came from the Caribbean itself.

As more people came to the Caribbean, there were more castaways living on the islands. Some of these were sailors who jumped ship. A few might have been shipwrecked. Others were runaway slaves, indentured servants, and convicts. And more were just disgruntled colonists who wanted to get away. They were a mix of French, English, Scottish, Irish, Dutch, and other peoples.

These island castaways became the first buccaneers. From the middle 1500s, they could be found on many of the islands, including Cuba, Jamaica, and Puerto Rico, but most of all on Hispaniola. (For more details on buccaneers, see page 54.)

A buccaneer holding his long-barreled musket with his hounds at his feet.

THE "TURTLE" SHELTERS THE BUCCANEERS

Tortuga is not much of a place—just a small island shaped like a giant turtle floating on the water (thus its name), located a few miles off the northwest coast of Hispaniola (an area that is now part of the country of Haiti). Despite its size, Tortuga's reputation has gone down through the ages as one of the greatest pirate strongholds of all time.

The location was good for pirates: it was close to the Windward Passage (between Cuba and Hispaniola), which became a main route for the Spanish ships. It was easy to defend: there were few places on the island where an enemy could land in force. Food and fresh water were plentiful: there were lots of animals to hunt and a profusion of yams, bananas, pineapples, and other fruit. On the nearby big island of Hispaniola, there were hordes of wild boars, flocks of pigeons, and semi-wild cattle abandoned by the Spanish. It was an ideal base for buccaneers. The Spanish rarely ventured to the northern and western shores of the island, preferring to stay near their city of Santo Domingo in the southeast.

The English first settled the island of Tortuga around the year 1630. The original village was attacked several times by the Spanish, who did not want foreigners living in their territory. Once, while most of the buccaneers were on Hispaniola hunting the semi-wild cattle, the Spanish launched an attack. The old men, women, and children of Tortuga were all slaughtered. Their bodies were left hanging as a warning to the buccaneers.

The Spanish also sent hunters to slaughter all the wild cattle on Hispaniola. They thought they could starve the buccaneers out and easily drive them away. Instead, they

Fort de Rocher, the Rock Fort built by Le Vasseur

got the opposite result. Angered by the killing of their families and the slaughter of the wild animals, the buccaneers thirsted for revenge. They turned to piracy and started attacking Spanish ships. The Spaniards had created their own worst enemy!

In 1642, Jean Le Vasseur, along with a band of one hundred men, arrived to claim Tortuga in the name of France. Finding the island sparsely settled (because the Spanish had run out most of the English), Le Vasseur quickly succeeded in making himself master of the island. Using his skills as a military engineer, he built Fort de Rocher (the "Rock Fort") on a flat-topped hill overlooking Tortuga's main harbor. He put twenty-four cannons in the fort. Protected by the fortress, a town quickly grew on the east side of the harbor. The town, called Basse-Terre, soon became a major center where buccaneers brought their dried meat, cowhides, and plunder.

Over the years, word spread about the settlement in Tortuga. Passing ships brought more and more recruits looking for freedom and a new start. These recruits included soldiers from the losing sides of wars, people looking for religious freedom, runaway slaves, people in trouble with the law, and escaped prisoners. They hated the Spanish, they hated bullies, and they swore to be free.

For a while, Le Vasseur ruled well, but power soon went to his head. His character changed, and he ruled as a sort of buccaneer king. He became vicious and greedy, and was very disliked. In 1652, he was killed by one of his own lieutenants in an argument over a woman.

Soon after, the Spanish decided it was time again to get rid of their unwanted neighbors in Tortuga. In early 1654, Spain sent a squadron headed by five heavily armed warships to attack the fortress. They landed several hundred men and eventually succeeded in taking Fort de Rocher.

With their fortress taken by the Spanish, the buccaneers fled to the larger island of Hispaniola. The Spanish, thinking they had solved the "Tortuga problem," soon withdrew. But they made a big mistake! They didn't leave soldiers behind on the island.

Within a few years, the French buccaneers not only moved back to Tortuga, but they also took over the western half of the island of Hispaniola as well. Their numbers and their strength grew. The Spanish would never get rid of them again.

"I SHALL ORDER CHAINS FROM FRANCE FOR THESE RASCALS!"

In 1665, King Louis XIV of France appointed Bertrand d'Ogeron as Royal Governor of La Tortue (French name for Tortuga) and of Saint Domingue (French name for Santo Domingo) in western Hispaniola, now the country of Haiti.

Bertrand d'Ogeron was a good man for the job. He had several years of experience in the New World. He had been a soldier, a trader, AND a buccaneer. He was known for his honesty, wits, and leadership. His abilities were quickly put to the test when he landed on Tortuga. There were a few people living in the town of Cayonne, on the west side of Tortuga Harbor. These were mainly the townspeople and merchants. Most of d'Ogeron's subjects were the cattle-hunting buccaneers, and they were scattered about Hispaniola, still living like savages. They were willing to let him be governor as long as he didn't bother them, though they generally ignored his laws.

D'Ogeron knew that as long as the cattle hunters roamed freely about the islands, there was no hope of governing them. His only chance was to get them to settle down. He encouraged them to become planters. Anyone wanting to build or start a plantation was given a loan at little or no interest (often from d'Ogeron's own pocket). He also came up with a clever method for getting some of his buccaneers to stop roaming. He exclaimed to a friend, "Corbleu! I shall order chains from France for these rascals!" And he was as good as his word.

Rumors spread throughout the area that the governor was planning something big, but no one was sure what it was. Finally, several months later, a French ship pulled into Tortuga's harbor. D'Ogeron quickly rowed out to meet it while curious buccaneers gathered on the docks to see what the governor was up to.

When the governor returned to shore, he had some Catholic priests with him. He announced that the ship was filled with single French women who had come to be brides for the buccaneers. The priests had come along to perform the marriages.

The buccaneers were very surprised and very eager to see the women. The men formed a half-circle on the beach. Using a small boat, the women were brought to shore in groups. Everyone remained quiet until the last group came ashore. The men came forward to meet the women. When each man found a willing bride, they were married on the spot by one of the priests.

With his "special tricks," d'Ogeron managed to increase the number of planters from 400 on his arrival at Tortuga to over 1,500 planters by 1669. He also encouraged the privateers to keep using Tortuga as a base, as he had no soldiers or navy of his own. He arranged to get letters of marque (official permits to plunder the enemy) for the sailors. The presence of the privateers gave them protection from the Spanish.

D'Ogeron did everything he could to increase trade. He managed to get many of the roaming cattle hunters to settle down and become farmers. Under the governor's guidance, tobacco, cacao, and sugarcane production had almost tripled. The privateers continued to have many successful raids against the Spanish and sometimes the English (with a certain percentage going to the French treasury, of course).

Bertrand d'Ogeron died in January 1676. They buried him in Paris. He is still regarded as a hero who civilized the buccaneers and laid the groundwork for the future country of Haiti.

ROGUES' HAVEN

The island of Jamaica was a valuable prize in the quest to see who controlled the New World and all its riches. The Spanish government did not recognize the value of Jamaica until it was too late. The English, on the other hand, quickly realized the value of this island. With its central location, it could be the key to the Caribbean.

Jamaica, discovered by Columbus in 1492, did not easily attract Spanish colonists. Its land was beautiful and rich, but not rich with the treasure the Spanish craved.

The Spanish were always on the search for gold and silver. Jamaica had neither.

Bands of buccaneers (mostly English, French, and Dutch outcasts and escaped indentured servants) began to roam the Caribbean, hiding out in the many bays and coves of the islands. Jamaica became a favorite hideout.

Even though Spain claimed all of the islands in the Caribbean, they never bothered to colonize most of them. Recognizing the advantages of having a foothold in the New World, other European powers started setting up colonies on a number of these islands.

However, until 1655, the Spanish had never lost any of their colonized land. The first territory taken from Spain was Jamaica. Taking Jamaica was not the original plan of the English. It came about as the result of bad leadership and the whims of fortune.

After the English Civil Wars in the 1640s and early 1650s, Oliver Cromwell (the new ruler of England) had many soldiers and warships on hand with nothing for them to do. To put these idle men and ships to use, he decided to start a campaign against one of the Spanish American colonies. He named this plan his "Western Design." It called for the British seizing Puerto Rico, Hispaniola, Cuba, and part of the Spanish Main.

The fleet left England in December 1654. Admiral William Penn (father of the founder of Pennsylvania) was the naval commander, and General Robert Venables was in charge of the army. Recruiting for the expedition didn't go well. The troops were mostly vagrants and prisoners. There were not as many volunteers as they had hoped. To make matters worse, after the expedition arrived in the Caribbean, tropical diseases reduced its numbers even more.

Even though Penn and Venables didn't have enough men, they had to do something to further Cromwell's Western Design. They chose Santo Domingo, the capital of Hispaniola, as their first target for attack.

It was a comedy of errors. They lost the advantage of surprise through delay. The untrained and undisciplined soldiers lacked weapons. Food and water supplies were low. To top it off, Venables and Penn argued over everything. The attack was a disaster.

They needed a new plan desperately. They could not return to England empty-handed or Cromwell could have their heads (literally)! They looked around for an easy target and decided on Jamaica, even though it wasn't on Cromwell's list. They knew Jamaica had no fort and few defenses. In May 1655, the British fleet entered Jamaica's deepwater harbor without a fight.

Though Jamaica was not part of his original plan, Cromwell recognized Jamaica's strategic value. He decided the island had to be held at all costs. Cromwell sent reinforcements. He even sent out a new governor because Penn and Venables had both given up and deserted.

Docks for English ships were built at the end of a long sandy peninsula that enclosed part of the harbor. A small town called Cagway grew up around the port. Fort Cromwell was built on the seaward side at the water's edge. Any ship entering the harbor had to pass within range of the fort's cannons. (There are no cliffs as shown in *Pirates of the Caribbean*, when Elizabeth Swann falls from the walls of the fort.)

The English worried that the Spanish would try to take Jamaica back. Believing a strong offense is the best defense, the English fleet attacked several Spanish colonies and captured many Spanish ships. By their attacks, the English kept the Silver Fleet of treasure galleons from sailing for several months. England's treasury swelled while Spanish revenues grew thinner.

Cromwell offered free land to anyone who would move to Jamaica. Word of Cromwell's offer spread, and settlers flocked to the new colony.

Charles II became king of England in 1660. To celebrate, the town of Cagway was renamed Port Royal. The fort got a new name too. It was renamed Fort Charles in honor of the new king.

As Port Royal grew, it became a thriving commercial center. Like most frontier boomtowns, Port Royal became known for its wicked and wild ways. This rowdy atmosphere attracted adventurers, various cutthroats, and especially the buccaneers.

Like Tortuga, Port Royal was a place that welcomed pirates—and their plunder. It was easy to bargain with carousing, drinking buccaneers, who were not skillful businessmen. Merchants flocked to Port Royal to take advantage of such "bargains." Silver and gold circulated freely. The merchants bought up the Spanish plunder (golden church ornaments, gold- and silver-embroidered cloths, rich silks, velvets, laces, and

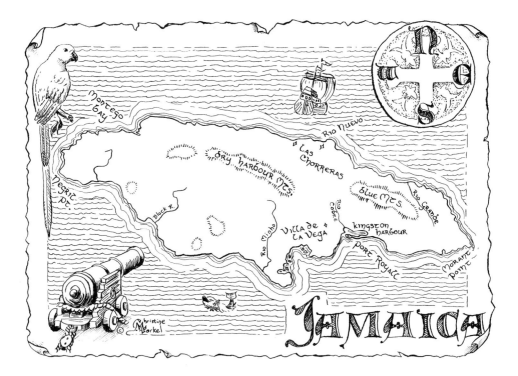

jewelry). The merchants shipped their "bargains" to England. On their return trips to Jamaica, they brought back English products.

Port Royal soon became known as a real party town. Taverns and grogshops were everywhere. More and more people were attracted by Port Royal's wild reputation and opportunities.

The English in Jamaica were constantly worried about attacks from the Spanish. In 1662, all but one of the warships were sent back to England due to economic cutbacks. Most of the army was dismissed. The citizens of Port Royal became afraid for their safety, so they worked out a plan. They invited the buccaneers of Tortuga (the French pirate stronghold) to come to Port Royal. The English offered the buccaneers letters of marque so they could attack the Spanish legally as privateers. The presence of the buccaneer ships would help give Jamaica the protection it so badly needed. It was a good arrangement for the buccaneers, too. Their ships could be repaired at the docks in Port Royal. They had a ready place to trade their stolen Spanish plunder. And there were plenty of places to enjoy themselves and spend all their loot.

The Tortugan buccaneers willingly took up Jamaica's offer. Many buccaneers (especially the English ones) readily moved to Port Royal and turned privateer.

Orders came from King Charles II to establish trade with the Spanish colonies, "even if by force." The Jamaican governor sent trade requests to the nearest Spanish colonies. As expected, the Spanish governors refused the requests. So the English chose their first target for "forced trade." It was Santiago de Cuba. Eleven privateer vessels (former pirate ships) and the one remaining navy warship, the HMS *Centurion,* went for a "visit." Their "trading mission" was very successful. They returned to Jamaica with half a million pounds of silver coins and other plunder.

The next year, the eleven privateer vessels and one warship visited Campeche in New Spain to "trade." They were successful but didn't find as much silver. They did, however, capture sixteen ships and several cannons.

The Jamaican privateers kept up the "trading missions" to the Spanish colonies. There was scarcely anyone on the island of Jamaica who did not benefit from these raids.

Anytime a ship was spotted returning to Port Royal, a celebration began. The fort's cannon fired a salute, and the townspeople came running. The king's officials were the first ones aboard to collect the king's tenth of the booty. Rum flowed freely, and the rest of the plunder was auctioned off.

Pirates and privateers flocked to the taverns when they came back from a successful voyage. Many spent their entire share of the booty in a single night.

Duels and drunken fights often made life in Port Royal more dangerous than life at sea. When the buccaneers were in port, they ruled the town. Few people were foolish enough to try to control the carousing buccaneers. Most of the townspeople were willing to put up with disturbance of the peace in trade for the riches that were pouring in and for the protection the pirates gave from Spanish attack.

This situation did not last for long . . .

CAPTAIN MORGAN WAS MORE THAN JUST A PICTURE ON A RUM BOTTLE

The most famous of all the Jamaican buccaneers was Henry Morgan. But don't go calling him a pirate. He always tried to play by the English rule of law. He never set out on an expedition unless he had a letter of marque giving him permission for what he did. Still, the Spanish certainly considered him a pirate.

Henry probably came to Jamaica as a young man with his uncle, Edward Morgan. They both came when the English first captured Jamaica. Henry was probably there on many of those attacks on Spanish colonies, all the time getting more experience and rising in rank.

In 1664, Governor Thomas Modyford of Jamaica got wind of a Dutch plan to attack the island. The governor decided to strike first. A fleet of ten ships and five hundred buccaneers led by Edward Morgan attacked the Dutch colonies on the islands of Curaçao, Saba, and Saint Eustatius. The attack failed and Edward was killed.

The Jamaican governor sent a second fleet against the Dutch two years later. This time Edward Mansveldt led the Port Royal privateers. Henry Morgan was one of his lieutenants. When Mansveldt was captured and killed by the Spanish, Henry Morgan was elected as "admiral" by the privateers.

As the leader of the Jamaican privateers, Morgan led many raids against the Spanish. By 1670, the Spanish were becoming bolder, and Spanish attacks on the English were increasing. Morgan was given the title of "Admiral and Commander-in-Chief of all the ships of war belonging to this harbor." Admiral Morgan's next feat was his most famous of all: the sack of Panama. Following this successful venture, Morgan returned to Port Royal a hero.

There was a problem, though. A peace treaty had been signed with Spain before the attack on Panama, but word didn't reach Jamaica until after Morgan had sailed. Spain threatened a new war with England if Morgan were not punished. He was arrested and sent to England as a prisoner in shackles. However, Morgan's deeds had so impressed those in high places, including the king, that instead of being imprisoned, he was knighted and sent back to Jamaica in 1674 as lieutenant governor.

Sᴿ HEN: MORGAN

Sir Henry Morgan

After the buccaneer victory in Panama, the Spanish forces in the New World were so weakened that Jamaica no longer needed protection from the buccaneers. King Charles II wanted peace with Spain and demanded a stop to all of the attacks. He decreed anyone attacking Spanish towns or ships would be considered a pirate, and pirates were no longer welcomed in Jamaica.

As lieutenant governor, Morgan worked hard to carry out the king's orders. He persuaded many of his former comrades to give up piracy. Some former buccaneers settled permanently on Jamaica as planters or craftsmen. Others joined crews of fishing or trading vessels, catching turtles or trading illegally with the Spanish colonists. Morgan hunted down those who kept up their pirating ways. They were sent to prison or were hung at Gallows Point near Port Royal.

Even though pirates were not openly welcomed in Port Royal, Jamaica remained a home for every kind of rogue. Pirates still turned up, but they came by the backdoor instead of the front.

After eight years as lieutenant governor, Morgan retired in 1682. He was a very wealthy man. But he spent much of his remaining years in the taverns with friends, talking about earlier days and their exciting deeds. He was often so drunk at the end of the night that his friends had to help take him home to his wife. He died in 1688 due to poor health from overdrinking.

Many of Morgan's former companions came to pay him their final respects. The governor at the time had spread word he would not arrest any pirates who came for the funeral. As Morgan's coffin was pulled through town on a cannon carriage, the warships in the harbor fired a twenty-two-gun salute in his honor (governors usually only got twenty-one-gun salutes). Morgan was considered quite a hero.

Pirates in the Movies: Sir Henry Morgan Returns to Jamaica

The 1942 movie *The Black Swan* has one of the best portrayals of Sir Henry Morgan (played by Laird Cregar). In the story, he has freshly returned from England, knighted and appointed governor of Jamaica (yes, he was actually only lieutenant governor, but this is the movies). He convinces most of his former privateers and buccaneers to settle down to lawful occupations, with a few major exceptions. Some of the worst "pirates" he deals with are actually the upper-class citizens of Jamaica.

DO YOU HAVE THAT SINKING FEELING?

Four years after Sir Henry Morgan's death, disaster struck Port Royal. In 1692, a comet was sighted by Edmund Halley, and it was named for him. You may have heard of Halley's Comet. People thought the comet meant bad things would happen. Later that year, just before noon on June 7, a powerful earthquake struck Jamaica, followed by a powerful tsunami. Port Royal had been built on sand, and two-thirds of it sank into Kingston Harbor. Two of the forts ended up underwater. Only Fort Charles remained on dry land (and can still be seen today). More than two thousand people died in Port Royal. Another thousand were dead on the remainder of the island. Many ships were sunk or wrecked in the harbor. The HMS *Swan* was washed out of the harbor by a big wave and thrown on top of a building. For days and weeks afterward, dead bodies floated in the harbor, making a horrible stink. More people died over the next few weeks because of injuries from the earthquake or from starvation and disease. The remaining survivors moved to the other side of the harbor and founded a new town called Kingston (now the capital of Jamaica).

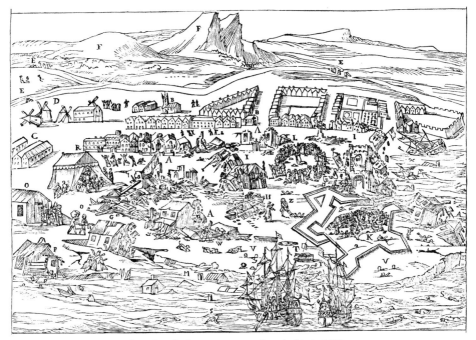

Port Royal after a strong earthquake hit in 1692.

As if one devastating earthquake wasn't enough, what remained of Port Royal was hit again and again by disaster. In the next couple of decades, fires, hurricanes, and earthquakes discouraged people from rebuilding. Today, Port Royal exists only as a sleepy little fishing village.

START PLANTING OR LEAVE!

Toward the end of the 1600s, the buccaneers were no longer welcomed in the Caribbean. Their main havens of Tortuga and Port Royal were settling down and becoming civilized. The buccaneers were encouraged to come ashore and become planters. If they didn't want to do that, they had to move on and find new waters.

Those who moved on also moved on to other prey. No longer were they just after the Spanish. The buccaneers were becoming outright pirates, going after ships of any country. No one was safe from pirates. They were becoming "villains of all nations."

THERE WASN'T SO MUCH GOLD IN THE GOLDEN AGE

As pirates spread out from the Caribbean in the 1690s, the "Golden Age of Piracy" began. It was the time of the big names in the piracy game: Captain Kidd, Blackbeard, Bartholomew Roberts, Samuel "Black Sam" Bellamy, "Calico Jack" Rackham, and the famous women pirates Anne Bonny and Mary Read.

The world had opened up. Trading ships carrying valuable cargos were going vast distances. European companies had been formed to trade with India, China, and other Asian nations. The English East India Company (also called the East India Trading Company) was formed in 1600. The Dutch East India Company was founded a couple of years later, followed by Danish, Portuguese, French, and even Swedish East India Companies. Their merchant ships often carried cargoes of cotton, silk, indigo, spices, tea, and opium. These were tempting targets.

The sea rogues were no longer just after Spanish silver and gold. They would take what they could get, wherever they could get it. Though this era was called "The Golden Age," gold was very hard to find. Pirates often came away with common items like some casks of rum, a few bales of cotton, and some dried fish.

This Golden Age did not last very long. Navies were getting stronger and patrolling more. The various East India Companies put pressure on their governments to clamp down on the pirates. Many pirate crews were captured, tried, and publicly executed (usually by hanging). Soon, most of the pirates had either been captured or disappeared ashore to avoid capture. By the end of the 1720s, piracy had been mostly wiped out—at least for several decades.

BECOMIN' A PIRATE AND KEEPIN' THE CODE

P irates have been with us from ancient times and are still active today. You don't have to sail the high seas to be called a pirate. A pirate can be someone who comes ashore to pillage and plunder, or who sails along the coast, in a harbor, or even along rivers.

The words "pirate," "buccaneer," and "corsair" are often used interchangeably, but that's not necessarily correct. In fact, depending on the era and the location, pirates have been called by other names. Many of them are listed on pages 54–56.

Often, one person's pirate was another person's patriot, depending upon your loyalties. For example, Sir Francis Drake and Sir Henry Morgan were heroes to the English but were *piratas* to the Spanish. John Paul Jones was an American hero of the Revolutionary War, but at the same time, the British considered him a pirate.

No matter how the word is used, a pirate is usually someone who flouts the rules of general society and does things his (or her) own way. Many pirates were cruel people who did awful things. Some were just petty thieves. Some were outcasts from society, just trying to make a way for themselves. Others were rebelling against unjust laws and governments. A few of them could even be considered heroes.

HOW PIRATES BECAME PIRATES

Why become a pirate in the first place? You might want to escape a life of slavery or the harsh life of a sailor on a naval or merchant ship. As a pirate, you usually got better quality food and could drink anytime you wanted (as long as the rum held out). You might be seeking adventure and a way to make your fortune. On a pirate ship, there were no schools nor baths, and you would have your mates protecting your back. This was quite an attractive prospect for a young lad with no other future in store.

There were several ways to become a pirate—

Start your own crew: Pirate crews were often created by several men getting together and deciding to "go on the account" (go pirating) together. If none of them already had a ship, they would steal one.

Mutiny: When a large part of a ship's crew plotted to take over the ship, it was called mutiny. It usually happened in the middle of the night. They killed or captured the captain and other officers. Any surviving officers and loyal crewmen were usually left behind on land or put into a small boat to fend for themselves on the seas.

Volunteer: If pirates captured a ship, the captured crewmen were often given the choice of joining up with the pirates or being released. If their captain had been treating them badly, or the food given them was bad or not enough, many would take up the pirates' offer. There were usually plenty of volunteers, so pirates often did not have to force common sailors to join them.

Be forced: If you were a carpenter, surgeon, musician, or sailing master, and pirates captured your vessel, you were in trouble. Pirates often needed these skills. The pirates might give you the choice, "Join with us and sign the articles . . . or die!"

Look for a pirate crew: You could head for some notorious port such as Port Royal or Tortuga. If you frequented the local taverns, you might pick up rumors about ships or crews with a "questionable" reputation that you might approach about joining.

Or you might hear someone was signing on a crew to go "on the account." They wouldn't openly say it of course, but they would probably imply what was up, if they thought they could trust you . . .

THEY WERE MORE THAN GUIDELINES

Most of the people who eventually became pirates didn't start out that way. Originally they were sailors, indentured servants, or workers in some menial job. But they got sick and tired of the brutality and mistreatment they received at the hands of others. They were tired of other people running their lives. They had seen how people who got put in charge (like officers and captains) could often be cruel and mistreat people under them. But no more! Things were going to change!

The pirates knew they needed some rules, though. They were a bunch of hardheaded, strong-willed characters, and they would be at each other's throats if they did not agree on how they were going to live together. For a bunch of rough men in rough circumstances, they came up with some pretty good rules for getting along together. Some of their rules were forerunners of modern democracy.

Pirates all voted on the rules together and then set them to paper. These rules were called articles. The articles told how the plunder would be shared out, how things would be decided on the ship, and what punishments people got for specific crimes. They even included arrangements for things like accident insurance in case they got injured.

Everyone who wanted to be a part of the crew had to agree to and sign the articles. They usually had a little ceremony. There was lots of celebratory drinking. Everyone swore an oath of loyalty, promising never to cheat or betray his shipmates. Then they signed the piece of paper with the rules on it. They signed it in a "round robin," a circle around the edges of the paper. That way, if they were caught later and the authorities found the articles, they couldn't tell who was the leader of the bunch. They would all be equally guilty.

On Bartholomew Roberts' crew, they signed the articles at night in the ship's cabin. By candlelight, the men could see on the table a platter with the articles and a loaded pistol. Most of them figured this meant they could chose between the two.

The oath was sometimes taken on a Bible, but there are other stories of pirates swearing on crossed pistols, swords, axes, a human skull, or astride a cannon.

As soon as a sailor signed the articles, he was a full member of the crew. But not everyone joined willingly. Some people with special skills (surgeons, navigators, carpenters, and musicians, for example) were forced to sign the articles under threat of death. Many such skilled people were believed at trials when they testified

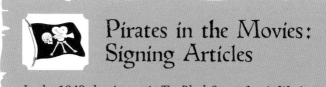

Pirates in the Movies: Signing Articles

In the 1942 classic movie *The Black Swan*, Jamie Waring (Tyrone Power) is shown signing the articles as he joins up with Captain Leech (George Saunders).

they were forced to join the pirates. As the articles had everyone's name signed to it, the pirate crew did not want the articles to fall into the hands of the authorities upon capture. If a pirate crew thought they were going to be taken prisoner, the pirates tried to destroy the articles. Because of this, only a small handful of articles are known about today.

BARTHOLOMEW ROBERTS' ARTICLES

ARTICLE I. Every man shall have an equal vote in affairs of moment. He shall have an equal title to the fresh provisions or strong liquors at any time seized, and shall use them at pleasure unless a scarcity may make it necessary for the common good that a retrenchment may be voted.

> *Every man gets a vote in major decisions. Every man can help himself to the food or alcoholic drink at any time, unless supplies were running short (which did happen a lot). Then the crew might vote to ration their supplies to make them last longer.*

ARTICLE II. Every man shall be called fairly in turn by the list on board of prizes, because over and above their proper share, they are allowed a shift of clothes. But if they defraud the company to the value of even one dollar in plate, jewels, or money, they shall be marooned. If any man rob another he shall have his nose and ears slit, and be put ashore where he shall be sure to encounter hardships.

> *In turn, every crewmember would eventually get a set of clothes. This was in addition to their fair share of the plunder.*

If any pirate took any extra treasure, even just one dollar, the punishment was marooning. (Pirates were called "marooners" because of their use of this punishment.)

If the offender robbed only from another pirate's personal belongings, they slit his ears and nose (so others would know not to trust him). Then he was set ashore in a place where things would be tough for him.

ARTICLE III. None shall game for money either with dice or cards.

Whenever there was gambling and wagering, there were winners and losers. Winners would be happy to have won someone else's money. The loser would not be happy and might start to think the winner cheated somehow. Pirates were smart enough to know this often led to fighting between crewmembers. Fighting between crewmates meant they were less likely to be successful pirates.

ARTICLE IV. The lights and candles should be put out at eight at night, and if any of the crew desire to drink after that hour they shall sit upon the open deck without lights.

Roberts thought that by requiring the men to drink on deck in the dark, they might not drink so much. It probably didn't make much difference. Most pirate crews did not have this rule.

ARTICLE V. Each man shall keep his piece, cutlass and pistols at all times clean and ready for action.

The crewmembers had to keep their weapons clean and ready to go at all times. This rule was rarely broken. Pirates were very proud of their weapons, very much like some people are with their cars.

ARTICLE VI. No boy or woman to be allowed amongst them. If any man shall be found seducing any of the latter sex and carrying her to sea in disguise he shall suffer death.

Pirates knew if there was a woman on board, there soon would be fighting over her. The punishment was DEATH for any pirate caught sneaking a girlfriend on board disguised as a man. They were very serious about this!

If a woman was being held prisoner, a guard was set over her to protect her from the crew until her ransom was paid.

Of course, there were some exceptions to this rule; we do know of some woman who became pirates. However, these were tough women who could take care of themselves. They had to use their strong wills and force of character to get the male crewmembers to accept them. (For more on women pirates, see page 107.)

ARTICLE VII. He that shall desert the ship or his quarters in time of battle shall be punished by death or marooning.

During battle, if a pirate left his assigned job, or left the ship, he would be killed or marooned. Pirates would not tolerate cowards.

ARTICLE VIII. None shall strike another on board the ship, but every man's quarrel shall be ended on shore by sword or pistol in this manner. At the word of command from the quartermaster, each man being previously placed back to back, shall turn and fire immediately. If any man do not, the quartermaster shall knock the piece out of his hand. If both miss their aim they shall take to their cutlasses, and he that draweth first blood shall be declared the victor.

Fighting was forbidden on ship. If two crewmembers had a quarrel with each other, they had to wait until they could go ashore.

On the beach, they would have a duel with pistols and swords. The quartermaster was in charge of the actions. When the quartermaster gave the word, the duelers turned and fired at each other. If a man did not shoot (or if his pistol misfired, which happened with flintlocks a lot of the time), the quartermaster knocked the pistol out of that man's hand. The duel would stop at this point if one of them was hit, and the other would be the winner. If both missed, then they would fight with their cutlasses. The first to draw blood won the duel.

ARTICLE IX. No man shall talk of breaking up their way of living till each has a share of £1,000. Every man who shall become a cripple or lose a limb in the service shall have 800 pieces of eight from the common stock and for lesser hurts proportionately.

The pirate crew set of goal of 1,000 pounds (that funny L stands for a pound sterling, a British value of money). They agreed no one would even talk about breaking up the group until they reached that goal.

If anyone got hurt along the way, they got a payment of 800 pieces of eight (or less, depending on how badly hurt they were). This was an early form of accident insurance.

ARTICLE X. The captain and the quartermaster shall each receive two shares of a prize, the master gunner and boatswain, one and one half shares, all other officers one and one quarter, and private gentlemen of fortune one share each.

> *This gives the formula on how to break up the plunder into shares. The captain and quartermaster got twice as much as a common sailor. Other officers got between $1\frac{1}{2}$ and $1\frac{1}{4}$ shares.*

ARTICLE XI. The musicians shall have rest on the Sabbath Day only by right. On all other days by favour only.

> *The musicians got to rest on Sundays. On Monday through Saturday, they were required to play music anytime someone asked them.*

Pastimes for Scurvy Dogs

WRITING YER OWN RULES

N ow that you've seen an example of actual pirate articles (and our own, on the next page), you might want to get together with the rest of your crew and see what kind of articles you can come up with. Your "crew" might include your brothers and sisters, or a bunch of your friends, or the kids in your class.

Pirates may have been outlaws, but they weren't stupid. They knew what it was like to be aboard a ship for months at a time. And they knew what they were up against. So they carefully chose the minimum rules they thought they needed to live by.

Your rules should be designed to help you all get along. You all get treated equally, you all do your jobs, and you all work together as a team to make the voyage a success. Remember, the articles will apply to ALL of you equally, no exceptions (pirates never tolerate favoritism).

Decide among yourselves just WHICH rules you think you need to get to your goal.

Once you've got them all agreed to, get yourself a big sheet of paper, preferably some parchment, and write 'em out big and proud. Remember, these are YOUR articles.

Cap'n Michael says:

Jamaica Rose an' I realized we'd never gotten around to writin' our own articles. So we sat down and put together a list of the rules we thought were most important to us . . .

PIRATE'S CODE

(Well, they be more like guide-lines, actually.)

All facial hair shall be unkempt and mangy.
(We've got standards, ya know.)

No songs about scurvy.

No frolikin' in the bilges.

One pet per pirate, parrot preferred.
(A kraken is not a pet!)

No relievin' yerself from the crowsnest.

No sword shall be larger than Cap'n Michael's.

Prisoners must be tied to something.
(No exceptions!)

Cannons should be tied down, too.
(No loose cannons.)

Prisoners should not be tied to cannons.
(It makes the prisoners irritable and the cannons hard to load.)

Cannons shall not be fired at Will.
(Unless you know for sure which one is Will.)

All boots should be black and scruffy.
(Unless yer bare feet already look that way.)

Swabbing will be done weekly.
(Whether it is needed or not.)

Tropic of Cancer & Tropic of Capricorn:

The Tropics are imaginary lines around the globe. The Tropic of Cancer is north of the equator, and the Tropic of Capricorn is south of the equator. Between these lines there is at least some time of the year when the sun will be straight overhead at noon. This region between the Tropics is like a belt that wraps around the Earth, centered over the equator. It has a very warm climate with lots of rain. This zone has no real seasons, so it is like summer all year long. In this region is where you find tropical jungles.

CROSSING THE LINE

You often have to go through some kind of ritual or test when you join a group. You are not a full member until you do. You are just a trainee or greenhorn. But once you go through an initiation ceremony, you officially become a member of the group.

Sailors of many lands had some sort of rite or ceremony whenever they crossed over an important landmark or area of the sea.

The ancient Phoenicians made sacrifices to their sea god whenever passing through the "Pillars of Hercules" (Straights of Gibraltar).

The Vikings had some sort of trial for new sailors. It often involved dunking in the water or being towed behind the ship for a length of time in the cold water. This was to see if you were tough enough to be a Viking. If you survived this test, you were worthy of being a member of the crew.

The idea of a ritual to please the gods and a trial to test the new sailors were combined together in the ritual of "crossing the line." This line might be the Tropic of Cancer, Tropic of Capricorn, or the equator.

The "crossing the line" ceremony could get pretty rough back then, because it tested the new sailors. The crew wanted to make sure the new sailors were tough enough to endure their first long sea voyage.

Not only did the "crossing the line" ceremony test a new sailor's endurance, but it also helped unite the crew together as a band of "brothers." This was important if the crewmen were to depend on each other in battle or against the power of the sea.

For a pirate or buccaneer, "crossing the line" of the Tropic of Cancer on the way to the Caribbean was important. The line marks where the tropics start. In the area of the Caribbean, it lies just north of the northern coastline of Cuba. It was celebrated with a ceremony that changed a landlubber into a member of the Brotherhood of the Coast. Crossing the Tropic of Cancer meant you were not only crossing an invisible line on the map, but it also meant the pirate ship was entering into the waters where the "fishing" was best: where they were most likely to find the treasure-filled Spanish galleons.

The privateer Captain Woodes Rogers (who later became governor of New Providence, an island in the Bahamas) used a common ritual called "ducking at the yard arm."

It was also a common punishment. It was simple, yet symbolic. He wrote in his log book on September 25, 1708, "This day, according to custom, we duck'd those that had never pass'd the Tropick before. The manner of doing it was by a Rope thro [through] a Block from the Main-yard, to hoist 'em above half way up to the Yard, and let 'em fall at once into the Water." He further added, "This prov'd of great use to our fresh-water Sailors, to recover the Colour of theirs Skins, which were grown black and nasty." It seems that the dunking in the water must have removed a few layers of dirt.

YOUR INITIATION INTO THE PIRATE BROTHERHOOD

After you and your friends have decided on the rules you'll live by and written them down as your articles, you need to sign them. Signing the articles should be a solemn occasion. You are committing yourself to stand by your pledge NO MATTER WHAT until the voyage is done. Or until you all agree to break up the crew. Once you sign your name, there is no backing out.

In the old days, they might pledge themselves with one hand on a skull, a sword, or some other weapon. They would drink toasts and pledge to stand by each other. Because, after all, if you won't stand up for your shipmates when they're in trouble, then who will stand up for you?

If you are forming a new pirate crew, then you should have a group ceremony—at night, perhaps, around a roaring fire, maybe at the beach or some other appropriately secluded location. It should be a private thing, just within the brotherhood, with no one else around except for some grownups to help you watch the fire. Each person pledges, and then they sign the articles. Remember to sign your names "Round Robin" style, around the edges of the paper, in a circle.

Later on, when you take new crewmembers into your ranks, have another signing ceremony. Let them know what a proud crew they are signing on with and what you expect of them. Just remember, it works both ways. You should NEVER ask anyone to do anything you wouldn't be willing to endure yourself. The "Golden Rule" is a very important thing to consider when you're surrounded by heavily armed pirates.

THAT'LL TEACH 'EM

Pirates knew they needed rules and consequences to live by in order to get along. The articles spelled out many of the crimes and punishments. The buccaneers and pirates used other punishments that were not mentioned in the articles.

The quartermaster dealt with minor crimes right away. If the crime was something major, the crew met and decided on the lousy dog's fate together.

No Matter What You Call 'em,
THEY'RE STILL PIRATES!
Various Terms for Pirates

Adventurer: A soldier or sailor of fortune available for hire. A mercenary.

Barbary corsairs: Pirates and raiders who sailed from North African ports along the Barbary Coast. This area now consists of the countries of Morocco, Algeria, Tunisia, and Libya. Barbary corsairs were mostly of the Islamic faith. (See *corsairs*.)

Boucaniers: Originally these were NOT pirates, but savage French cattle hunters who roamed the island of Hispaniola. Their name comes from their method of smoking and drying meat, called *boucanning*. The local Indians taught them how to do this on a wooden grill over a slow fire. When the Spanish tried to drive these hunters out of Hispaniola through various attacks, the *boucaniers* took to the sea. They turned into vicious pirates, attacking mostly Spanish ships. (See *Buccaneer*.)

Brotherhood of the Coast (or Brethren of the Coast): A loose union of the Tortugan, Jamaican, and Cuban pirates and privateers. They lived by a strict code called the "Custom of the Coast" where they shared booty equally, voted on all major decisions, and knew each other by first names only. Their code was MORE than "just guidelines."

Buccaneers (in Spanish, *Bucaneros*): English form of the French word *boucanier*. Originally, cattle hunters turned pirate. They could be English, French, or sometimes other nationalities. These days, people often use the word (somewhat incorrectly) to refer to any kind of pirate. (See *Boucaniers*.)

Cimaroon: An African slave who had escaped from the Spanish. They lived in the wild forests and mountains of the Caribbean islands. The word means "dweller in the mountains." Others say the name comes from the Spanish word *cimarron*, meaning "wild." Some of these escaped slaves joined up with the buccaneers and became pirates. (See *Maroon*.)

Corsairios Luteranos: Spanish term for the Protestant French sea raiders (pirates and privateers).

Corsairs: Pirates or privateers who mostly sailed in the Mediterranean Sea in oared galleys. (See *Barbary corsairs*.)

Diablos: Spanish for "devils." One of the names the Spanish called the hated foreign buccaneers intruding on the lands claimed by the Spanish.

Filibuster: An English buccaneer. This is the English version of the French word *flibustier*, which is the French version of the English word "freebooter," which was a version of the Dutch word *vrijbuiter*. The word is also used for the tactic of pirating or hijacking a debate in Congress (but then, many people consider politicians to be pirates anyway).

Flibustier: French buccaneer. French variation of "freebooter." The name has nothing to do with swatting flies, though they were great pests in the tropical islands.

Fraternité de la Côte: French name for the Brotherhood of the Coast.

Freebooters: A buccaneer or pirate. This word is the English version of the Dutch word *vrijbuiter,* meaning plunderer or pirate. It comes from the words for "free" and "booty."

Gentlemen of Fortune: Another term for an Adventurer.

Guardacosta (also Costa Garda): Privateers of many nations hired by local Spanish governors to keep out foreign traders. (See *Interlopers*.) They earned their money by selling the prizes (ships) and cargo they captured. The Guardacosta were often very cruel and tortured the English, French, and Dutch merchants they caught.

Interloper: An illegal trader trespassing on a trade monopoly. Trading companies (such as the East India Company) carefully guarded their trade arrangements. They chased off independent traders. Interlopers were often called pirates, even when they weren't (though sometimes they were). The term can refer to a person or the ship they use. Eventually the word came to be used for someone who is a busybody or meddler.

Ladrone: A robber, thief, or pirate. For a while, the Mariana Islands were called the Ladrones Islands (Islands of Thieves). When Ferdinand Magellan visited the islands on his round-the-world trip, the natives stole one of his boats, hence the name.

Maroon (or Marron): A runaway slave, or one of his offspring, who formed villages in the forests and mountaintops of the larger Caribbean islands. Maroon is a shortened form of the word "cimaroon." (See *Cima-roon.*) Not to be confused with the verb "to maroon," or Marooner. [First mate Nick in the movie *Swashbuckler* portrays a maroon who has joined the pirates.]

Marooner: A pirate of the 1600s and 1700s. This comes from their practice of abandoning (marooning) people on barren islands as punishment. Marooning was the custom of putting the offender on shore on some wild or uninhabited cape or island. They would leave him stranded with a gun, a few shots, a bottle of water, and a bottle of powder. If they were being really mean, they would leave the person on a bare sandy island, where there was nothing to hunt or eat but perhaps fish, if they were lucky. If things got bad enough, the stranded person might use the pistol on himself to end his misery.

Peirates: Greek word for pirate. It comes from the word *peiran* meaning "attack." This is the root for the word "pirate."

Pechelingue (also Pechelingua): Spanish term for Dutch Caribbean pirates and privateers in the 1500s and

1600s. It was sometimes used to mean pirates of any nation. (See *Vrijbuiter*.)

Picaroon: A pirate or a pirate ship. English version of the Spanish word *picaro*, which meant rogue or adventurer.

Piratas: Spanish word for pirates, but also used by the Spanish to refer to all foreign seamen (whether pirates or not) who sailed in the New World.

Privateers: Basically, pirates with permission. These were "legal pirates" sailing under a letter of marque. Letters of marque were special papers granted by a governor or ruler that allowed the privateer to plunder ships of enemy countries. Privateers made their money by selling the ships and cargo they captured, but they had to give part of the plunder to their country's treasury. These permits were only recognized by the country that issued them and by their allies. If captured by the enemy, a privateer was usually treated as if he were a pirate. Clouding the issue, pirates often had fake letters of marque and claimed to be privateers. The term can also refer to the privately owned ship used on privateering missions.

Rover: A pirate or his ship. Comes from the German term *rauber,* meaning robber. (See *Sea Rovers*.) Not to be confused with dogs named Rover, even though some pirates were Sea Dogs.

Scummer: A nickname for a pirate or buccaneer first used in the late 1500s. This refers to a person who scours the sea.

Sea Beggars: Dutch pirates or privateers of the late 1500s. They are named for the Beggars of the Sea, a rebel group of Protestant seaman during the Revolt of the Netherlands in 1569. They were forerunners to the Zee-Roovers.

Sea Dogs: English privateers and pirates during the reign of Queen Elizabeth I. They were a mix of pirates, explorers, naval commanders, slavers, traders, and adventurers. Even when they did not have prior permission to attack Spanish ships and colonies, Elizabeth usually approved. The most famous were Sir Francis Drake and Sir Walter Raleigh. These days, the phrase means an experienced sailor. [The movie *The Sea Hawk* shows a good example of Elizabethan Sea Dogs.]

Sea Rovers (Zee-Roovers): 1. Dutch privateers and pirates attracted by the wealth the Spanish were finding in the New World. (See *Sea Beggars*.)
2. A term for a pirate of any nationality, mostly in the Caribbean. Comes from the German term *Seerauber*, meaning sea robber.

Swashbuckler: A rough, noisy, and boastful swordsman in the 1500s. He carried a small round shield (a buckler), which he swashed about while fighting, and made a lot of noise on it with his sword. Swashbucklers tended to swagger about town and be bullies, sort of like hoodlums. Swashbucklers were generally not pirates.

Turkish Devils: Another term for Barbary corsairs.

Vikings: Norse explorers and pirates who plundered and colonized many areas of northern and western Europe from the late eighth to the early eleventh century.

Vrijbuiter: A Dutch privateer. (See *Freebooters*.)

For major crimes, pirates resorted to a few "special" punishments.

FLOGGING

The most common official punishment was flogging. This was a beating with a whip, switch, or strap. While all the crew stood and watched, the man was stripped to his waist and tied to the mainmast or the capstan. Sometimes he was tied across the back of one of the cannons (that was called "kissing the gunner's daughter"). He would be hit across his bare back with a whip or a lash. Sometimes they used a special whip called the "cat o' nine tails."

The "cat" was a rope whip of nine strands covered with tarred knots. "Letting the cat out of the bag" refers to the ritual removal of the cat o' nine tails from its special red carrying bag. The cat was also called "the captain's daughter," because it was used only on his command (not to be confused with the "gunner's daughter").

Pirates enjoy a game of "Monk Polo" as they flog their steeds (captured monks) with cat o' nine tails.

Since many pirates had served as sailors, they had often felt the "kiss of the captain's daughter." Because of those bad memories, many pirate crews did not use the cat o' nine tails. But some did, and even overdid it. William Watkins tried to run away from Bartholomew Roberts' ship in Africa. As a punishment, he received two lashes from every man in the company. This was at a time when Roberts had more than one hundred men on his crew!

MAROONING

We discussed Marooning on page 55. Often the guy being marooned was left in a place where, if he were clever enough and lucky enough, he might survive on his own. But if the guy did something really horrible, the pirates might leave him on a sand bar—one that became submerged at high tide. Or . . .

ONE MAN ISLAND

Often with no land in sight, the accused was thrown overboard with a plank on which to float until either sunstroke or sharks had their way.

HOW TO DEAL WITH MURDERERS

This was a "special" punishment that pirates had. If a pirate murdered a fellow pirate, he was often dealt with this way: He would be tied facing his victim's body. Extra weights were attached to him, and he, along with his victim, was dropped overboard. The last thing he saw was the face of the man he had murdered.

MESSAGE IN A BOTTLE

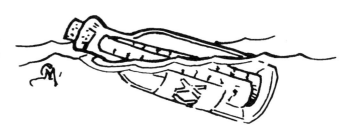

Have you ever walked along the beach or along a river and found a bottle with a message in it? Imagine opening the bottle and reading a message for help from a person shipwrecked on a deserted island! Maybe even a message from a marooned pirate!

If you put a message in a bottle and send it down a river or throw it out on the ocean waves, what are the chances someone will find it and send you a message back?

People have been sending messages in bottles for a long time. The earliest recorded instance was by an early Greek scientist, Theophrastus. Around 300 BCE, he sent messages in bottles to study the currents of the Mediterranean Sea.

Throughout time, there have been many reasons people have sent messages in bottles. Some sent messages asking for help and rescue. Others wanted to study the currents of oceans and rivers to see where the bottles would go. And some just did it for fun to see how far their bottle might travel and who might answer their greeting.

There was one case where a man was captured by mutineers (called pirates by some people) and was rescued because of a message in a bottle. In 1875, there was a mutiny aboard the *Lennie* after it set sail from England. The mutineers murdered the officers. They spared one of the stewards because he knew how to navigate while none of the mutineers did. The steward was brought on deck and ordered to sail to Greece. But he tricked the mutinous crew by taking them close to the French coast, and then telling them they should wait there for better winds. While they waited, the steward and a cabin boy quickly wrote messages about their dire situation and put them into bottles. Then, when no one was looking, they dropped the bottles into the ocean. Soon a French Navy vessel found one of the bottles. They found the *Lennie* and boarded it. The surprised mutineers were arrested. Four of them were eventually executed. The steward and the cabin boy were safe, and they owed it to a message in a bottle.

Now, would you like to write a message in a bottle and see if anyone finds it? You could use some of the "antique paper" you made (see page 114).

USING A MESSAGE IN A BOTTLE

HOW TO SEND A MESSAGE IN A BOTTLE

Things You'll Need:

† Paper
† Pen
† A clean bottle, preferably two-liter size
† One dollar bill
† Cork (optional)
† Envelope (optional)
† Forever stamp (optional)

Write your message. Remember, you are writing to a stranger to see if they will answer you. Tell them a little about yourself, but not too much. Remember, pirates were careful.

Add your address in case someone finds your bottle and wants to answer you. Or put in your email address. You could get a new email account like Yahoo (it's free) just for this purpose. You just need to check it every few days. (Talk to Mom and Dad to see which method they would prefer you use.)

After your letter is written, it's time to put it into the bottle. Use a large two-liter bottle—a large bottle is easier to spot and it's less likely that some sea animal is going to swallow it. It's best to use a clear bottle. A green or other color of bottle makes it harder to see your letter inside. Also, take the label off to make it easier to spot your letter.

Is your bottle empty? If not, finish drinking what's inside. Wash the bottle out so it's not sticky. Then let the bottle dry upside down. You wouldn't want your letter to get soggy, now would you? That could make it hard for someone to read it if the letters get all blurry.

If you want the person who picks up your bottle to write you back in the mail, you could also include a stamped and addressed envelope. Use a Forever Stamp on it, so if it takes a long time until someone finds your bottle, the stamp will still work, even if postage rates have gone up. (If you want the finder of your bottle to send you an email message, then you won't need an envelope or stamp.)

USING A MESSAGE IN A BOTTLE

(Continued)

Roll up your letter (together with the envelope if you are including one). Tie some ribbon or string around it so it won't unroll. If your paper rolls open inside the bottle, then it would be hard to get it out again. You can use a pen to roll the paper around to get it nice and tight.

If you really want someone to spot your message, then let's increase its chances of being found. You've used a large two-liter bottle, so that already means it will be easier to spot. And you've removed the label, so it's easier to see the letter inside. Now, before you slide your rolled up message into the bottle, wrap a ONE-DOLLAR BILL around it before you tie it with the string.

If someone spots a soda bottle with a one-dollar bill in plain view inside, they are a lot more likely to pick it up, don't you think?

Now slide your rolled up message, with the dollar bill wrapped around it, into the bottle. Put the cap back on, nice and tight, so no water will get in. Finally, take your bottle to a lake, river, or the ocean, give it a kiss for luck, and toss it in.

INVITATION IN A BOTTLE

If you are throwing a pirate party, then a great way to invite your guests in style is to send them a message in a bottle.

You will need:

† Plastic bottles, 12–20 ounce size, one for each person
† Corks that fit the bottles
† Address labels
† Rolled-up scroll invitations tied with ribbon
† Stapler
† Ribbon, string, or twine
† Something to add: coins, jewels, sand, shells, etc.
† Funnel (for sand)

> Ahoy Shipmate!
> Yer invited to a
> SKULL AND
> CROSSBONES
> PARTY!
> Onboard the (name of your ship)
> (your address)
> on (date) at (time)
> Come dressed as a pirate!
> RSVP . . . or else!
> Signed: Captain (your name)

Prepare your invitations as described on page 117, but do not add a wax seal or the invitations might not fit into the bottle openings.

Use plastic bottles with the labels removed. Plastic water or soda bottles should work well. Wash the bottles out well and give them time to dry.

Use the funnel to add an inch or two of sand to each bottle. Don't put in too much sand or it will hide your message. Add a couple of seashells and a doubloon, or a jewel could be included too. If the weather is warm, don't use chocolate coins, because they might melt and make your invitation hard to read.

Make sure the scroll is rolled tight enough to fit through the opening of the bottle. Tie the scroll tightly with one end of an 8-inch length of ribbon. You do not want your scroll to open up inside the bottle or your guest will never get the invitation out! Make a knot in the other end of the ribbon. Staple the knotted end to the side of the cork.

Seal the bottle with the cork.

Address the label, including your return address, and attach to the side of the bottle. Make sure it sticks down completely. Now hand-deliver your bottles to each of your invited guests. What fun it will be when your friend pulls out the cork, and the message comes out with it.

And here's a game you can play with your guests using the bottles.

BOBBING FOR BOTTLES

Things You'll Need:

† Parchment paper notes written with tasks
† Ribbon or string
† Small, clear bottles with lids (plastic water bottles work great), at least one for each guest
† Large tub of water

Write a different task on each piece of parchment paper. Some examples are
Make noises like a monkey.
Walk the plank—balance on a board and walk to the other end.
Hop like a peg-leg pirate all the way across the yard.
Swab the deck—wash the patio with a mop.
Stack twelve doubloons in a single tower without them falling over.

A few notes will tell where rewards or treasure are hidden.

Roll up the notes and tie them nice and tight with the ribbon. If they come undone and unroll in the bottle, it will be hard to get them out.

Float the closed bottles in the tub of water. Your guests will take turns getting one of the bottles out of the tub of water—but hands must be kept behind their backs. They have to get the bottle with their teeth! Once they have a bottle, they will read the note and then do what it says. If they successfully complete the task, they get a piece of eight.

DRESS LIKE A PIRATE

YOU BET YER BRITCHES!

In movies and television you've seen a lot of examples of how pirates were "supposed" to look. Unfortunately, a lot of times these landlubbers get it completely wrong! We're going to show you how pirates really looked. We've got three notorious pirate captains, including Blackbeard himself, to show you what a well-dressed pirate was all about.

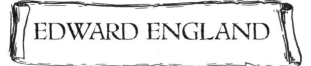
Cockade: An ornament of folded ribbon, sometimes worn on the hat instead of a feather.

Tricorne: A hat with three sides folded up. Usually the point goes in front, but sometimes pirates wore them backward just to be cool.

Neckerchief: Scarf tied around the neck (not just for Boy Scouts).

Coat with lots of buttons: Deliberately not buttoned up. Who's got time to do all those buttons?

Boarding axe: Not only can you hack with it, you can stab as well! Boarding other vessels and stealing their goods is what it's all about.

Sash tied around the waist: A handy place to stow yer weapons. Some sashes were long enough and wide enough when unfolded to be used as an impromptu stretcher to carry you if you were wounded (or dead).

Breeches: Sounds better than calling them shorts.

Stockings: Worn on your legs to keep the mosquitoes from biting. They look cool with short pants—er, uh, breeches.

Name: Edward England

Dates: active as a pirate from 1717 to 1721

Country: England

Ship: *Fancy*; *Pearl*; *Victory*

Flag: His Jolly Roger was the classic design of a skull above two crossed bones on a black background. Eyewitness accounts say he was "flying a black flag with a skull and crossed bones at the main." Other pirates were described using the same design, including Samuel "Black Sam" Bellamy and John Taylor.

Best known for: Captain England, a pirate with a conscience, was generally kind to his prisoners. England was fairly successful as a pirate, sailing mainly along the coasts of Africa and Madagascar, and in the Indian Ocean. His favorite targets were slave ships. It was reported that he captured more than fifty of them off the west coast of Africa. Pirates liked the slave ships. They were large, stocked with provisions, and well armed with cannons. They were perfect for converting into pirate ships. The slaves were often recruited to become pirates.

Unlike many other pirates of his day, England did not kill prisoners unless it was absolutely necessary. This ultimately led to his downfall, when his crew mutinied against him because he refused to kill sailors from the *Cassandra*, an English trading ship. He was marooned on Mauritius and died shortly thereafter in 1721.

Name: Major Stede Bonnet

Alias: "The Gentleman Pirate," also used the name Captain Thomas

Dates: active as a pirate from 1717 to 1718

Country: Barbados

Ship: *Revenge*; *Royal James*

Flag: His flag showed the skull for death, a dagger showing he is ready to fight, a heart for the sorrow he will bring, and a bone to show that his victims might die at any time. This design may be a fanciful artist's idea, for an eyewitness only said he flew a "Death's Head."

Best known for: Major Stede Bonnet was an unlikely pirate. He was a rich and successful plantation owner on the island of Barbados, described by his neighbors as "a gentleman of good reputation and estate." But one day, something snapped, and he decided he was going to be a pirate. He immediately went out and bought a sloop (see page 105), which he named the *Revenge*, and hired a crew of seventy men (including some pirates) to man her. Some say a nagging wife drove him to it. Whether or not that was true, he did leave shortly afterward in the middle of the night without saying goodbye to Mrs. Bonnet. In 1717, he met up with the infamous Blackbeard, who invited Bonnet to come aboard Blackbeard's ship and stay awhile as a "guest." Placing one of his officers aboard Bonnet's ship as captain, Blackbeard added Bonnet's ship to his fleet. For a while, Bonnet was a virtual prisoner aboard Blackbeard's ship. Eventually, Bonnet was given his ship back, and they parted ways. Soon after, Stede Bonnet was captured off the coast of Cape Fear, North Carolina. He was hanged for piracy on December 10, 1718.

STEDE BONNET

Wig: Keeps your head warm.

Black ribbon: To tie up the loose ends of your wig.

Tricorne under the arm: Even if you don't want to wear a hat, you can still look important carrying it around.

Long, pleated coat: Slits in the back allow your sword to poke through.

Wide cuffs on the sleeves: Some of them had buttons on them to discourage you from wiping your nose on your cuffs.

Rapier in scabbard: A long skinny sword. Not as intimidating as a cutlass, but a lot lighter to carry around.

Musket: A long rifle. You can pick off your enemies from a distance. Great way to get rid of that pesky captain on the other side.

Glaring eyes:
To intimidate enemies.

Burning slow match[†] stuck under the hat:
"I like the way it wreathes me face in smoke and gives me that proper devilish look." (Warning: Kids, don't try this at home. It's a great way to catch your hair on fire and you won't enjoy it when your parents beat out the flames on your head.)

Baldric: An over-the-shoulder belt for holding weapons. Usually made of leather. Sort of like that sash Miss America wears, only a lot more practical.

Four flintlocks in holsters attached to the baldric.

Scruffy, long beard matted in dreadlocks.

Another baldric.

Two more flintlocks in holsters hanging from a baldric. Flintlocks only had one shot, and it took a few minutes to reload, so pirates would carry more than one.

Belt.

Cutlass: A short curving sword worn here in a scabbard.

Two holsters for even more flintlocks: Either Blackbeard was a really bad shot, or he expected a lot of enemies to gang up on him at the same time.

Rifle: As if he didn't have enough weapons on him already.

Trousers: Worn by some pirates instead of those short sissy breeches.

Buckle shoes.

† **Slow match:** *Cotton cord soaked in a gunpowder water solution to make it smolder for hours. It was used to light cannons.*

Name: Captain Edward Teach

Alias: Blackbeard; also Edward Thatch or Thach; John Drummond, (a recent biographer claims his real name was Edward Beard)

Dates: active as a pirate from 1716 to 1718

Country: England

Ship: *Queen Anne's Revenge; Revenge; Adventure*

Flag: His flag showed the devil holding an hourglass (indicating to his victims that their time had run out) and stabbing a heart from which three drops of blood have fallen. This was truly a fearsome flag for one of the most feared pirates of all time.

The only eyewitness account of Blackbeard's flag we know of said Blackbeard flew a "Death's Head." It is possible he had more than one flag.

Best known for: He was one of the most famous pirates of all time. He was described as being 6 feet 4 inches tall with a long, scraggly black beard tied with red ribbons. Before attacks, to terrify his victims, he lit slow matches and put them under his hat. They surrounded his whole head in a wreath of smoke that smelled like sulfur (rotten eggs).

Pastimes for Scurvy Dogs

THERE'S A PIRATE IN YOUR CLOSET

To get that proper piratical look right away, you don't need to spend lots of your hard-plundered doubloons on a ready-made costume. You can probably make do with what you can find in your closet (or maybe Mom or Dad's closet, but be sure to ask first). You will also need a little imagination.

The easiest outfit to construct is that of a simple pirate sailor or pirate lass. If you are very clever, you might also put together a fancier pirate captain's outfit by using some of these tricks.

THERE'S A PIRATE IN YOUR CLOSET

(Continued)

SIMPLE PIRATE SAILOR

First put on some up-to-your-knees plain-colored or striped socks. If you or someone in your family plays soccer or Little League, the uniform socks should work great. If no one in your family plays these sports, then plain dark men's dress socks should do the trick.

Next come the pants. Find a pair of plain-colored baggy pants or loose sweat pants. It's best if you can find a pair without zippers. Also, avoid pants with pockets you can see. Sweatpants usually have a drawstring, which is perfect for our needs, and they usually don't have visible pockets.

Try to find pants that are a basic color: blue, brown, green, red, or black would be good. Avoid bright colors like fluorescent orange or lime green or hot pink.

First, you need to "blouse" them at or above the knee. To do this, turn them inside out. Put your feet into the bottom of the leg opening (instead of through the waist opening as you normally would).

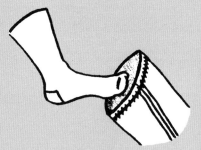

Put pants leg on inside-out, foot first.

Pull the leg opening up to your knee. Attach it with a big rubber band, a cord, or a thick ribbon. Make sure it's not too tight! There is a major artery going down the back of your knees. If you cut off the blood flow to your legs for too long, your leg may have to be amputated and replaced by a wooden peg leg. True, this would do wonders for your pirate look, but it sure would make the rest of your life a lot harder.

Once you have both ends of the pants legs tied just below your knees, grab the waistband of your pants and pull them up to your waist. They now should be right side out, hanging a little below your knees, and puffed out a bit. Very simple, no? Now you have instant old-timey-looking knee breeches.

Next up is a piratey-looking shirt. If there is

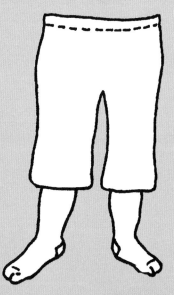

Knee length pants and socks.

an old white dress shirt nobody in your family minds if you cut up, this is best. It is fine if it's a little big for you. Cut off the cuffs and pull a dozen or so rows of threads out. This is called "unraveling." It will give your sleeves a raggedy worn-out look.

Sleeve folded in to hide the cuff.

Sleeve cut off with a ragged edge.

If you need to keep the shirt in good shape and can't cut it up, then shove your sleeves up your arm to just below your elbow. Tie them in place with a cord, ribbon, or rubber band. Let the baggy part of the sleeve hang loosely over the ties to hide them. Again, make sure your ties are not too tight, or you will end up like Captain Hook.

Don't bother to button up the front of the shirt. Instead, take the front shirttails and tie them into a knot just at your belly button. Tuck the back of your shirttail out of sight into the rolled-

Simple Pirate Sailor—complete outfit.

under hem of the shirt. Fold the collar of the shirt in so it looks like you have no collar. At the same time, roll the front opening of the shirt in to hide the buttons and buttonholes. Easy peasy!

For the finishing touches, see if you can find a couple of brightly colored scarves or scraps of cloth. They can be the same color or different colors. Use the smaller piece as a headscarf.

Tie the longer piece around your waist as a sash. Tie it so the knot is on your side, by your hip. If it's so big the ends hang down on the side, that is fine. If the ends drag on the floor, though, wrap it around your middle two or more times to take up the extra length.

The waist sash serves a few purposes. Besides adding some color and style to your outfit, it hides any belt loops or zipper your pants might happen to have. It also gives you a place to tuck your dagger or sword, if you have one.

For your feet, try to find some plain sandals. Leather ones without any modern decorations are good. Or you might wear some plain canvas slip-on shoes with no socks. Lace-up sneakers should be your last choice.

You might use some face paints or Mom's mascara (with permission, of course, if you don't want to eat gruel for a week) to make a moustache, or make lots of little brown or black dots around your chin for beard stubble.

Basic Pirate Lass—complete outfit.

BASIC PIRATE LASS

Girls have more options. They can decide to dress as a pirate sailor and be a girl in disguise. In that case, follow the directions for the Simple Pirate Sailor outfit above. If you prefer to be a pirate lass, follow the instructions below.

Starting with the blouse, see if you can find a light-weight pullover top with no buttons or buttonholes in front or back. Loose puffy sleeves are best. If you have a top like this, it can be worn pretty much as is.

For your skirts, find two long skirts. They can be of different lengths but should be at least below your knees, if not longer. They should be two different colors. The fabric should be solid colors, or one of the skirts could be striped or plaid. Avoid prints, but if you have to use a print, a small floral or geometric design is best. (See pages 68–69 under the pants discussion for color ideas.) A pirate lass can get away with a brighter color than a lad might. No bright neon colors, though.

Put both skirts on, with the longer one underneath. The blouse should be hanging loose over them. Do not tuck it in. Find a simple belt, preferably a black leather one with a big buckle. Put the belt around your waist, on top of the blouse. Then bring up the bottom hem on one side of the outside skirt and tuck it into your belt. This will show off the bottom skirt.

You can wear the same type of socks as the Simple Pirate Sailor, or you might wear a pair of plain-colored tights.

Your footwear can also be the same as the Simple Pirate Sailor, or you might wear some plain Mary Jane or China Doll type shoes (black is preferable). Find something with low or no heels. Avoid modern decorations on your shoes.

To complete your outfit, tie a scarf around your head. Add some hoop earrings or bangle bracelets, and you are done.

(Thanks go to Francisco, the Spanish Pirate, for teaching us how to find a pirate in our closet.)

BEHIND EVERY SCAR IS A REALLY GOOD STORY: SPECIAL EFFECTS MAKEUP

Your clothes, hat, sword, and other props are just part of getting the look of a pirate. You might not have thought of it, but your skin can also be part of the costume.

Remember, pirates led a rough life. They didn't bathe much, if at all, other than the occasional dip into the water. Their skin was tough and leathery from being out in the sun all day, even if they were young. They were very likely to have acquired at least a few scars. They might even have some fresh wounds.

You can really have fun creating these special effects on yourself. Add to the fun by having a really good story to tell about how you got each scar.

DIRTY AND LEATHERY SKIN

Give yourself a "tan" on all skin that is exposed. Face paints can work well for a short time, if you are not getting too hot and sweaty. (We recommend Snazaroo face paints: www.snazaroo.com.)

For a longer-lasting effect, you might ask your Mom (or any other female relative) if she has any makeup she's willing to let you use. Add some charcoal from a fire and you are ready to "dirtify."

First, wash your face and hands. Yes, you need to remove the real dirt before we add the "dirt." Otherwise, the makeup won't stick very well.

Use a makeup sponge (ask Mom if she has any of these, or get a pack of them in the makeup section of a general store or drug store).

Using the sponge, apply the face paints or makeup in the same way you would add polish to shoes (if you've never polished shoes, then just put a little on the edge of the sponge and apply it in small overlapping circles). Layer the colors to get a grimy, dirty, filthy look. Use a few different browns, one about the same color as your skin, and a couple of shades that are darker than your skin. Start with the lightest color first, around most of your face (but not around your eyes). Circle your eyes with a darker brown. Be careful not to get

(Continued)

it in your eyes. Blend around the edges of the two colors.

Put the darker color in the hollows of your cheeks (to find the hollows of your cheeks, open your mouth like you are screaming, and the areas of your cheeks where there is no bone behind them are the hollows). You can also experiment with some purple, dark blue, and grays in the darker areas of your face.

Figure out where face creases would be. Wrinkle up your face like you are squinting in the bright sun and see where your face creases. Put a darker color in these creases. Blend the edges between the darker colors and the lighter colors.

After you have finished with the other colors, get some charcoal dust on your fingers and apply smudges here and there.

Also, don't forget to "tan" and "dirtify" the skin on your neck and hands and other places where your skin will show.

For a better, longer-lasting look, you'll have to spend more coins on professional quality makeup. Here's how to create a pirate look with professional makeup. Pick either a cream or cake foundation for your basic layer. (Cream/grease: Ben Nye. Cake Foundation: Kryolan, Ben Nye, Mehron, or Joe Blasco.) On top of the foundation, use character powders from Ben Nye or Mehron to add dirt. Character powders cling to your skin yet wash off easily. The color "Plains Dust" looks like real dirt. "Ash Powder," also known as "Fullers Earth," offers a dust tone. "Charcoal Powder" can create grease stains or powder burns from firing a pistol.

Before you go to bed, be sure to wash off all of your makeup. Use cold cream or makeup remover (skin lotion might work in a pinch). Plain soap and water by itself does not work very well.

Sources for Professional Makeup:

Theater/costume stores
http://stageandtheatermakeup.com/
http://www.stagemakeuponline.com/

DIRTY FINGERNAILS AND TOENAILS

Of course, a pirate has the grimiest hands of anyone. Not only does he never wash his hands, but he also gets black powder stains, tar stains, and grease on his hands. Yuck! Use liquid-based black makeup to stain under your fingernails and around the edge of the fingernail. Do the same with your toes if your feet are bare. Also stain the cracks and wrinkles of your hands. Warning: It will be a few days before your fingernails look clean after this. You can use a fingernail brush to get the worst of it off.

BRUISES

Bruises can be created with the right mix of colors and thorough blending. Use professional foundation colors (listed above) applied with a makeup sponge. Violets and reds deepened with black make realistic fresh bruises. Older bruise areas should be surrounded with yellows. Keep the color and shape uneven since blood doesn't spread evenly around a bruised area. Use the lighter color for the outer edges, with the deeper maroon color in the center. To get uneven color, pat with your sponge.

SCABS AND CLOTTED BLOOD

You'll need some supervision from your parents while using the following chemicals. Dampen dark sawdust (such as walnut or mahogany dust; check with your local woodworking shop, perhaps at the high school) with professional adhesive thinner. Mix in professional prosthetic adhesive or spirit gum adhesive (from the makeup sources on page 72) until the mixture is the thickness of peanut butter. It will dry quickly, so apply it immediately to the skin. The "scab" will also hold firmly, even when wet, so remove it with professional adhesive remover (acetone or nail polish remover will work too, but it's hard on your skin). If you can't get the dark sawdust, you can substitute cornmeal, but you will need to color it dark brown with some drops of food color, using equal amounts of red, blue, and yellow.

SCARS

The experienced sailor or pirate would likely have a few facial scars. Use Rigid Collodion (found at the professional makeup supplies sources). With your parents supervising, simply paint a line or small area on your skin. It wrinkles the skin as it dries. Repeated applications will deepen the effect. The shrinking action causes the surrounding skin to pull inward for a very realistic scar look. A thick buildup of Rigid Collodion will create raised scars. Color these scars with dark beige foundations, or red and white professional foundations, depending on your skin tone. If you want the scar to look newer, use more reds and violets.

TEETH

Pirates probably didn't brush their teeth very much, if at all. They also tended to get scurvy, so many might be missing a tooth or two. Professional tooth black applied to one or two teeth looks startlingly real. To make your teeth look rotten and decayed, use teeth paint (from the professional makeup supply places).

BELIEVABLE BLOOD

FLOWING BLOOD

A stab wound from a dagger, a sword fight, or a punch to the jaw—you can create bloody wounds right before the eyes of your audience with real-looking fake blood! The following recipe makes simple, cheap, believable blood:

RECIPE 1: CORN SYRUP "BLOOD"

You will need:

- † 16 ounces light corn syrup
- † 1 ounce red food coloring
- † 1 ounce dishwashing soap
- † 1 ounce water

Mix ingredients. Store in the fridge until needed. This "blood" is extremely sticky and can stain skin and clothes, so make sure it's washed off quickly. Use a stain remover on clothes or wear clothes that you (or your parents) don't mind looking stained.

Adjustments: Add a drop of blue food coloring to create a more realistic color. Leave out the dishwashing soap if you want to make "blood" you can squirt out of your mouth. Adding condensed milk makes the "blood" less transparent and more like real blood.

RECIPE 2: CARDIFF RED BLOOD

This "blood" washes out of clothes better than the Corn Syrup "Blood" and can be used in the mouth reasonably safely (though don't swallow it if you can help it).

You will need:

† 1–2 teaspoons arrowroot (white powder used in baking, found in health food shops)

† 1 cup water

† Red children's nontoxic powder paint (get at an art or teacher supply store)

† Brown children's nontoxic powder paint, or coffee concentrate (make coffee concentrate by adding a small amount of water to coffee granules)

Add arrowroot to water heated on the stove. Stir continuously until the mixture gets thick and gloopy. Add a spoonful of red children's nontoxic powder paint and stir. (DON'T USE regular paint!) The mixture should be a bright red. Add a tiny amount of brown powder paint or coffee concentrate to darken the "blood" as required. Store in a container in the fridge. When needed, thin by adding more water to make the "blood" the right thickness. For bullet hits, you need to thin the "blood" quite a bit to allow it to spray out.

"BLOOD" PACKS

Corn Syrup "Blood" can be used to create instant stab and bullet wound effects. Pour "blood" into ziplock sandwich bags. As you fill, leave an air bubble in the top where the "blood" pack will be hit. This air bubble provides enough pressure to allow the pack to explode easily when it's supposed to. Zip the bags closed and then fold the openings over and seal them down with strong tape. Tape the "blood" pack under your clothing, and when your "injury" will occur, clutch the wound to explode it. For blood coming out of your mouth, use the smaller snack-sized ziplock bags (again, taped closed). Bite down on them to make them explode. You should practice these techniques ahead of time to get the right feel for exploding the bags.

TIPS: Keep your eyes open during the Halloween season. At that time, you can often find inexpensive versions of special effects makeup at your local drug store. At dollar and 99 cent discount stores, you can sometimes find cosmetic makeup really cheap. And sometimes you can get free makeup samples at makeup counters.

SHARP POINTY THINGS AND THINGS THAT GO KA-BOOM!

 pirate's weapons were among his most prized possessions. Picking the right kind of weapon and knowing how to use it could mean the difference between life and death. We will tell you about the different weapons the pirates used and give you the pros and cons on each one. So look them over and make your choice!

MY OTHER SWORD IS A CUTLASS: TYPES OF SWORDS PIRATES USED

A sword was the pirate's main weapon. He did have black powder pistols and maybe a few rifles or a blunderbuss. In the heat of battle, though, these were only good for one shot, and then he was reduced to using it as a club or as a secondary weapon to help fend off a sword blow. A pirate's sword was what he depended on, and pirates were very proud of their weapons. He may have been dressed in ragged clothes, but you can bet his weapons were clean, sharp, and ready for action. Weapons were also one of the symbols of his freedom. On merchant ships and military vessels, sailors were not allowed to own their own weapons. All they were allowed was their sailor's knife, with the tip broken off. All the rest of the weapons were locked up until the time of battle. But a pirate had his own weapons, which he kept with him.

Parts of the Sword

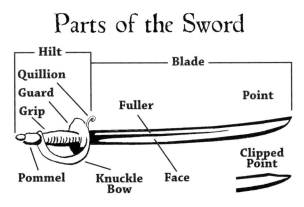

The types of weapons he carried depended on the era he lived in and his station in life before he became a pirate. Most pirates would have carried a short sword, called a hanger. There were many different kinds of hangers, but the one the pirates liked best was the cutlass.

CUTLASS

The cutlass was a single-edged short-sword with a short sturdy blade. The blade was usually slightly curved with either a standard or a clipped point. A cutlass is actually a type of hanger. The main difference is that a cutlass had some kind of knuckle guard (usually called a knuckle bow). The short curved blade of the cutlass made it ideal for use in the close quarters on board a ship. It was much less likely to get tangled in the lines and rigging, and the heavier blade could deliver a powerful blow. A pirate could stab with it, slash with it, and use it to knock a lighter one out of the way. In extremely close-quarters fighting, he could use the heavy guard like a set of brass knuckles and smash it into his opponent's face or body. It was a very versatile weapon, and a pirate didn't need as much training as he would with a rapier or small sword.

NOTE: In the Caribbean, even today, they call a machete a cutlass. A machete is just a big flat blade with a handle on it, used for hacking through the jungle.

HANGER

The hanger is a common (generic) name used for a variety of a single-edged military shortswords with a straight or slightly curved blade. They could have a knuckle bow like a cutlass or a simpler straight guard. A popular type had a curved guard on each side of the blade (called quillons), with a brass scallop shell attached to it, (as shown in the illustration). This was called a shell guard. If a man was in the military before he became a pirate, he might carry this type of weapon.

HUNTING SWORD

The hunting sword is the civilian version of the hanger and is mainly used for hunting. It was usually fancier than the hanger, with engravings such as hunting scenes on the blade and handle.

RAPIER

Former military officers, ex-noblemen, or men from the upper classes would carry a rapier.

This was the formal or court sword of the period. The hilts were sometimes extremely fancy and offered a lot of protection to the hand. These were popular until approximately 1700. After 1700, they would have used the small sword (except in Spain and Italy, where rapiers stayed popular for a long time). A rapier had a long, straight, slim blade. The blades were a lot longer than those on a cutlass; they started at 30 inches, with some up to 4 feet long! They were great for stabbing somebody from a long distance away but not very good at blocking a blow from a heavier blade like a cutlass. The rapier's longer blade would also get caught in the lines and rigging easier. It was not a very practical weapon on a ship unless the owner was a *really* good swordsman.

SMALL SWORD

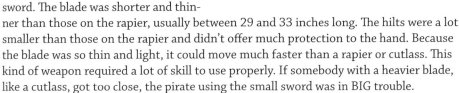

After 1700, the small sword replaced the rapier as the gentleman's or formal sword. The blade was shorter and thinner than those on the rapier, usually between 29 and 33 inches long. The hilts were a lot smaller than those on the rapier and didn't offer much protection to the hand. Because the blade was so thin and light, it could move much faster than a rapier or cutlass. This kind of weapon required a lot of skill to use properly. If somebody with a heavier blade, like a cutlass, got too close, the pirate using the small sword was in BIG trouble.

MAKE YER OWN FOAM CUTLASS

Would you like to make your own pirate cutlass so you and your ship-mates can stage pirate battles? We'll show you how to do it with just a few inexpensive materials.

What you will need to make two cutlasses:

† 6 feet of ¾-inch PVC pipe, cut into 2½–3 foot lengths, depending on how long a cutlass you want (found at hardware or home improvement stores).

† ¾-inch closed cell pipe insulation, aka "closed cell foam," at least ¾-inch thick (usually comes in 6 foot lengths; one 6-foot length is plenty).

† duct tape, comes in many different colors (DO NOT buy aluminum tape; it has sharp edges).

† open-cell foam (e.g., couch cushion, sponge, sleeping bag padding).

† grip tape, bicycle handlebar tape, or soft rope (optional).

† thick cardboard, leather, or closed cell foam camping mat (better) for hand guard (optional).

† hacksaw or PVC pipe cutter (hacksaw blades are sharp; ask Mom or Dad to help you with this part).

† utility or razor knife (razor knives are VERY sharp; ask Mom or Dad to help you with this part).

† sandpaper

Step 1: Cut the PVC with a hacksaw or pipe cutter to the desired length (Have Mom or Dad help you with this part.). Sand both ends of the pipe to remove any rough or sharp edges. Measure in 8 inches from one end of the pipe and mark with a permanent marker. Make a second mark 1½ inches from the end of the pipe (see Figure 1). This area will be the handle of your cutlass. (You can make the handle longer than 8 inches if you wish, but don't make it any shorter.)

Figure 1: Cut pipe and mark as shown.

Step 2: Starting at the end opposite the handle, slide the pipe insulation onto

(*Continued*)

the PVC until you reach the mark made in Step 1. Cut the insulation off flush with the end of the pipe so that no PVC shows past the end of the insulation (see Figure 2). This will be the tip of the cutlass. Leave at least 8 inches of PVC uncovered on the other end of the pipe (this is where the handle will be).

Figure 2: Slide insulation to 8-inch mark.

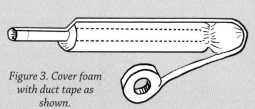

Step 3: Completely cover the foam with tape. To do this, anchor the loose end of the roll of tape on the handle of the sword (where there isn't any foam). Then run the strip

Figure 3. Cover foam with duct tape as shown.

of tape lengthwise along the length of the "blade." When you reach the tip, place a chunk of open-cell foam (about 4 x 4 inches) onto the tip of the cutlass. Run that first piece of tape up and over it without squishing it down too much. Then continue placing that first piece of tape down the other side back to the handle (see Figure 3).

Step 4: You just laid down a 5–6 foot strip of tape. Repeat taping on one side, up and over the tip, and back down the other side as many

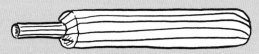

Figure 4. Keep taping until all foam is covered.

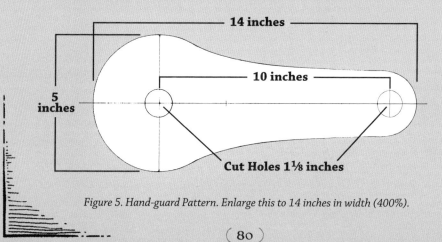

14 inches

10 inches

5 inches

Cut Holes 1⅛ inches

Figure 5. Hand-guard Pattern. Enlarge this to 14 inches in width (400%).

times as it takes to cover all of the foam. Be sure not to squish the cell foam at the tip any more than necessary to tape it. It should be at least as big around as the insulation and feel soft and squishy at the end (see Figure 4).

Take a pin and poke holes in the tape over the open-cell foam so that air can escape, making the tip softer and safer.

Step 5: Make a copy of the hand-guard pattern from Figure 5 using a copy machine. You will need to enlarge the drawing until the pattern is 14 inches wide. Many office supply stores have copy departments that can do this for you. Have them print it on 11" x 17" paper so the drawing will fit.

Or you can use the drawing in Figure 5 as a guide and create your own hand-guard pattern. Just make sure the holes are 10 inches apart and are a little over 1 inch in diameter (you can use the end of the PVC pipe as a guide). Use carbon paper to transfer this pattern to your hand-guard material. Carefully cut out the pattern using a utility knife. Cut the mounting holes slightly larger than the outside of the PVC pipe. (Have Mom or Dad help you with this part.) Check to make sure pipe will slip through the holes in the hand guard.

Step 6: Slide the handle end of your cutlass through the wide end of the hand guard. Slide it down until it touches the foam insulation. Tape that end in place. Bend the hand guard so it forms a U, and slide the narrow end of the hand guard over the handle. Leave approximately 1½ inches of PVC pipe showing past the narrow end of the hand guard; tape that end in place (see Figure 6).

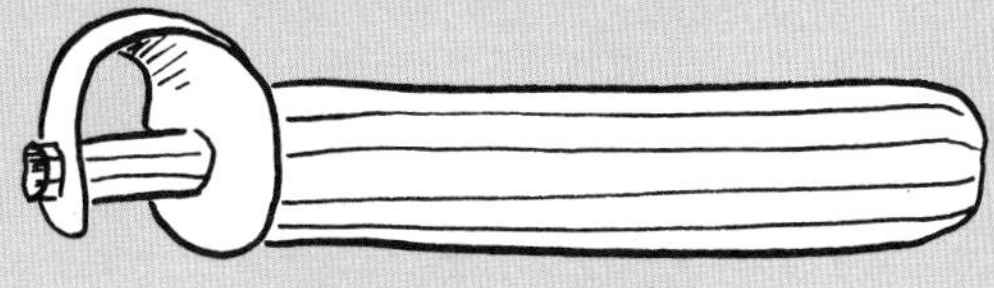

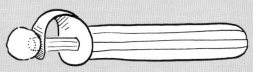

Figure 6. Bend hand guard as shown and insert over end of pipe.

Step 7: Place another chunk of open-cell foam (about 4 x 4 inches) so it wraps around the handle end up to the 1½-inch mark you made in Step 1 and wrap it with duct tape like you did the tip (see Figure 7).

Figure 7. Tape the handle end.

Wrap the area between the two ends of the hand guard with duct tape. This will make it easier to grip than plain PVC, which is slippery.

Or wrap the handle with soft rope, leather lacing, or bicycle handlebar tape to form a comfortable handle. This will give you a better grip and make it look better.

THE STEPS FOR A BASIC SWORD DRILL

Now that you've made your foam cutlasses, it's time to learn how to use them properly. Have you ever watched a sword fight on TV or the movies and wondered, "How do they do that?" They are actually swinging real swords at each other, but nobody is getting hurt (except the bad guy, of course).

What they are doing is called "stage combat." It's the art of making a sword fight look real, and doing it safely at the same time.

We are going to teach you the basics (some of the same techniques used by professional stunt men), so you can work out a sword fight routine of your very own. With a little practice, it will make you the envy of all your friends.

Now lets move on to your initial starting position . . .

NOTE: These positions are describing the movement from a right-hander's point of view. For you lefties out there, you will need to reverse everything.

EN GARDE

You should always start from the en garde position (on guard). Start with your body sideways to your opponent. Your right shoulder should point toward your opponent. Leave your left foot where it is and turn your right foot so it is pointing towards your opponent. Keeping your feet in that position, twist your body a little to the right so you are facing forward a bit, toward your opponent. The forearm and hand are parallel to the floor. Your right arm should form an "L" from your shoulder to your wrist, with the bottom of the "L" pointing forward. The point of your sword should be up and toward the opponent's eyes.

DEFENDING YOURSELF

The seven basic defensive (protective) parries are each designed to protect a different part of your body.

1ST PARRY: From en garde, move your forearm across the chest, with your wrist and hand turned down with the point of the blade down. This covers the inside of your body and left side (or right side if you are a lefty).

2ND PARRY: Your sword arm is brought back to the side of your body. Your sword hand is turned down with sword point down. This covers the right side of your body from the waist down (or left side for lefties).

 **3RD PARRY:** Your sword arm keeps in the same pose as the 2nd parry, but your wrist and hand turn up. Your sword point comes up. This covers the upper right side of your body.

 **4TH PARRY:** Move your hand to the opposite side of your body, covering the inside upper section and blocking an attack to your chest.

 **5TH PARRY:** Your upper arm is parallel to the ground from your shoulder. Your forearm is raised straight up. Hold your sword even with the top of your head and pointing across. This protects you from blows to the head.

6TH PARRY: From 5th position,  sweep your hand down from high to low across hip. Your hand should move to just below your hips.

7TH PARRY: This is a flashy move. Your hand moves straight up and even with the top of your head. Your blade tip points toward  your right (or left if a lefty). Your forearm should be pointing straight up. Your arm and blade take a window-like position. Your blade covers an attack to your head.

RULES OF THE SWORD: THE BASIC SAFETY RULES OF STAGE COMBAT

1. **KEEP PROPER DISTANCE:** The fighters should never be close enough to actually hit each other's body with the weapon. First, check the distance by having the attacker slowly point the sword toward the defender as an attack. The point should be more than 8 inches away from the defender.

2. **EYE CONTACT:** Eye contact should ALWAYS be made before the fight begins. Partners should ask each other "Are you ready?" and wait until he answers "ready" before beginning.

3. **PARRYING:** All parries (blocking your opponent's sword with your own) should start from close to your body and move outward. For example, if someone is attacking your left elbow, then your sword actually starts on the right side of your body and moves leftward to meet the attacking weapon. Think of it as pushing the other weapon away.

4. **AIM FOR THE BLADE:** Don't hit your opponent on purpose! The idea is to hit the other person's BLADE. Remember to keep your proper distance as you go through your routine, so if you make a mistake, you won't accidentally hit them.

5. **BE AWARE:** You should always look all around you before you begin to make sure the area is clear. Then keep an eye out after you begin in case anyone wanders into the area. You should always have adult supervision.

EVERY TOOL IS A WEAPON: DAGGERS, DIRKS, AND STILETTOS

SAILOR'S KNIFE

Every sailor had a sailor's knife. This was the sailor's all-purpose tool. The knife had a single-edged blade with a flat tip (merchant ship and Royal Navy captains would order the points snapped off of all the sailors knives so they couldn't use them for fighting). There was usually a hole in the end of the handle for tying on a rope lanyard. This was so you wouldn't lose it when working high up in the rigging.

DAGGER

This fighting knife with a long double-edged blade has a cross guard above the handle to help protect the hand. Although daggers are primarily a stabbing weapon, they could be used for either thrusting or cutting.

DIRK

The Scottish word for a short dagger, the dirk is a fighting knife with a single-edged blade (usually) and no cross guard. It's primarily a cutting weapon.

NAVAL DIRK

This had a longer blade than the standard dirk. It could be either single- or double-edged and had a cross guard. This was the dirk favored by midshipmen.

STILETTO

Stilettos were stabbing weapons. They were similar to daggers but had long, slim, unsharpened blades with sharply pointed tips. The blades were usually triangular in cross section but were sometimes round, square, or even diamond-shaped. This design was perfect for penetrating chain mail or other armor. It is a nasty weapon. If it didn't kill you immediately, it caused a wound that would not close properly. The victim usually either bled to death or died from the resulting infection.

BELT AXE

The smallest axe carried by sailors was the belt axe. This small axe fit readily in the belt and had a flat hammer–like face, called the poll, on the side opposite the blade.

BOARDING AXE

This was a larger axe, useful for repelling boarders and cutting away damaged rigging. Every navy had its own unique style of boarding axe. In combat, it was a lethal weapon, capable of killing a man with one blow.

GRENADE OR GRENADO

A small hollow iron ball filled with a mixture of black powder and other nasty shrapnel such as broken glass, rocks, or lead shot, it worked like a modern grenade but was a lot more treacherous.

BOARDING PIKE

A nautical spear with a flat leaf-shaped blade, it was used both for forcing your way aboard enemy vessels and for repelling boarders.

THOSE WHO LIVE BY THE SWORD GET SHOT BY THOSE WHO DON'T

Next to his cutlass, a pirate's favorite weapon would have been his flintlock. The pistol may have only fired a single shot, but that shot could be devastating. These weapons were not like the small handguns used today. They fired a big bullet, usually two to three times the size of one used in a modern pistol.

MATCHLOCK

The first black powder hand weapon was called a matchlock. This firearm used a lever with a burning cord attached to it. When you move the lever, it touched the cord to a pan full of explosive black powder. They may have been primitive, but they were reliable in dry weather. There were pistol and musket versions of these, though the pistols were rare.

External View of the Flintlock

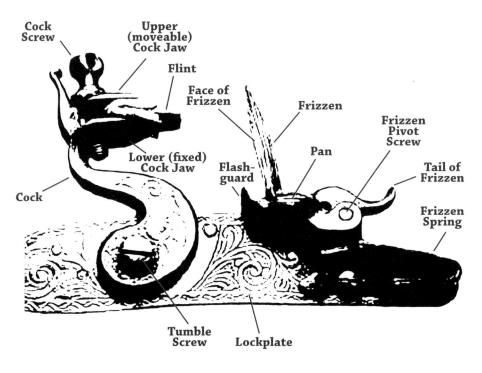

Cock Screw
Upper (moveable) Cock Jaw
Flint
Face of Frizzen
Frizzen
Frizzen Pivot Screw
Lower (fixed) Cock Jaw
Flash-guard
Pan
Tail of Frizzen
Cock
Frizzen Spring
Tumble Screw
Lockplate

WHEELOCK

A wheelock was easier to use than a matchlock and could be fired in bad weather. However, the mechanism was fragile and expensive to make, so they weren't very practical for warfare, especially onboard a ship.

SNAPLOCK, SNAPHAUNCE, AND FLINTLOCK

From the late 1500s to the 1800s, the black powder weapon of choice was the snaplock. This is a weapon that uses a flint hitting a steel striking surface to produce sparks. The earlier version was called a snaphaunce, but it was improved by making the striking surface a part of the pan cover. This improved version was the flintlock.

A French gunsmith invented the flintlock around 1610. It was the first handheld black powder weapon that was practical for use at sea. A flintlock uses a flint and a piece of steel called a frizzen to fire the weapon. When you pull the trigger, the flint flies forward and hits the frizzen. This makes a bunch of sparks. The frizzen flies open and the sparks go down into a little pan full of powder. The powder catches fire. The fire goes through a little hole in the side of the pan and into the gun barrel. There is more powder inside the gun barrel. When the fire hits the powder, it explodes and pushes the bullet out the end of the barrel and at your target.

This all happens very fast. You get a flash, a loud BOOM, lots of smoke, and the thing you were aiming at now hopefully has a BIG hole in it.

There are many different kinds of flintlocks, but most people had one of three different types:

PISTOL

A pistol was usually the best weapon for a pirate to carry. A pirate could shoot it with one hand, and it was small enough that he could carry several. The bad thing about them was there was only one shot, and they were not very accurate. A lot of them had a brass cap on the butt end, so after a pistol was fired, it could be turned around to make a good impression on people (used as a club).

MUSKET AND LONG GUN

A musket had a long barrel like a modern rifle, but the inside of the barrel was smooth (unlike the spiral inside a modern rifle barrel). Pistols were only accurate to ten yards. Muskets were accurate up to one hundred yards! The long barrel meant it took two hands to fire, and it was a lot harder to carry than a pistol, but it was great for shooting someone who was far away.

BLUNDERBUSS

The blunderbuss was the shotgun of the period. The name comes from the Dutch *donderbuss*, which means "thunder gun." The end of the barrel flares out like a funnel or trumpet. Pirates could pour lead pellets, rocks, broken glass, or just about anything small into the barrel, and then fire it at someone. It was a nasty weapon. It was only accurate up to twenty yards, but within that range, it was deadly. Nobody wanted to be on the front end of a blunderbuss.

Cap'n Michael says:

Remember—a flintlock is NOT a device to keep your flint from being stolen.

LAND OF THE FREEBOOTERS

In the late 1600s, pirates in the New World were looking for new havens to sell their plunder, to relax, and to repair their ships. The pirate ports of Tortuga and Jamaica were getting "civilized," and pirates were no longer welcomed.

At the same time, American colonists were paying very high prices for trade goods from England. The laws required they only buy from and sell to British merchants. They weren't allowed to trade with merchants from other countries to get better prices. On top of the high prices set by the merchants, lots of taxes and tariffs were added. It was "highway robbery" for the colonists!

To get around the high prices, the American colonists often welcomed trade with smugglers and pirates. In fact, they preferred to deal with pirates. The pirates sold their ill-gotten goods cheaper than the smugglers. And while in port, the pirates were big spenders. The shopkeepers and tavern owners got richer whenever the pirates were around.

The governors of some American colonies invited the pirates to use their ports and harbors. Some governors accepted bribes to give the pirates free run of their seaports. In places like Rhode Island, Pennsylvania, and the Carolinas, pirates had safe places where they could fix their ships, find new crewmen, and sell their goods when they returned to port.

Pirates in rich gaudy silks walked the streets of New York City. They were welcomed in the city. True, piracy was still officially illegal, but gold and silver given to officials caused them to look the other way when pirate ships sailed into New York harbor and crates of stolen goods were unloaded onto the docks. The local merchants lined up to buy the plunder. Prices were MUCH better than buying the lawful goods brought from England.

In his official reports to England, Governor Benjamin Fletcher wrote of how he was getting rid of the pirates in New York. At the same time, he accepted bribes from pirates and was good friends with at least one of them—Thomas Tew (see page 143).

In time, the welcome mat for pirates was removed as England replaced corrupt pirate-loving governors with more law-abiding ones. In 1698, Fletcher was called back to England in disgrace. At the same time, the British navy stepped up the patrols that were looking for ships smuggling goods.

Many of the pirates moved on to new retreats.

Cap'n Michael says:

Arrr . . . I always knew that politicians were pirates at heart.

PIRATES, PATRIOTS, OR MOBSTERS

fter the end of the "Golden Age of Piracy" (1650s–1720s), most pirates decided it was better to earn an honest living as privateers. With plenty of wars going on during this time, there were lots of opportunities to get some loot through privateering. Plus, the British Navy was patrolling more heavily, making it much riskier for pirates. Piracy had almost died out in the Caribbean and American waters after the 1720s.

Then, in the early 1800s, there was another little flurry of piracy. The American Revolution was over and a new nation had been formed, one that did not have much of a navy to patrol her waters. Soon, Spanish colonies in Central and South America were following the example of the United States by declaring independence from Spain. All of this turmoil and change created opportunities for those who weren't too fussy about how they made a living. Around the waters of the Gulf of Mexico, there were many smugglers, privateers, and pirates. It was often hard to tell the good guy from the bad.

THE BROTHERS LAFITTE

Into this mix came the Lafitte brothers, Pierre and Jean. To the citizens of New Orleans, the Lafittes were "Robin Hoods" of the swamps. They used the swamps to smuggle things in through the "back door" of New Orleans rather than through the "front door" of the Mississippi River. Their swampy kingdom was called Barataria.

In many ways, the Lafittes were the original American mobsters. If you wanted something and weren't too choosy about where it came from, they were the ones to see. They smuggled goods difficult to get through legal sources, often at much better prices. When it was made illegal to import slaves to the United States from other countries, plantation owners had a hard time getting enough slaves. Jean and Pierre were happy to help. They smuggled in slaves from the Caribbean Islands.

Pierre, being the older brother, probably made most of the business decisions. He lived in New Orleans and met with the business people there. Jean was younger, more handsome, and took more risks than Pierre (though many of the stories about Jean were really things Pierre did). Jean traveled between New Orleans and their headquarters on the islands of Grand Isle and Grand Terre, where he could oversee their business. These neighboring islands were on the coast just west of the mouth of the Mississippi River. This is where they kept most of the smuggled goods and slaves, guarded by their trusty men, the Baratarians. They also had warehouses in New Orleans itself.

Jean was often seen in the streets and parlors of New Orleans, and many times was a guest of the wealthy citizens. He was said to be quite a dashing gentleman, very handsome and very admired by the ladies. Yet, to the new American government, he was nothing but a bandit and a pirate.

Name: Jean Lafitte

Dates: Born ca. 1778 and died ca. 1823 (or possibly later)

Country: France and Louisiana, United States

Ship: The Lafittes had many ships, often a small fleet, but the best known were the privateer *La Diligente*, the brig *Dorada*, *Amiable Maria*, *The Pride*, and the *Presidente (Petit Milan)*.

Flag: Before 1810, the flag of a French privateer; after 1810, the flag of Cartagena (Colombia), claiming he had a commissions as a privateer. Lafitte was also said to have flown a solid blood-red flag, and the yellow, blue, and red tri-color of Venezuela when he moved to Galveston.

Best known for: His life as a privateer and for helping win the Battle of New Orleans, thus saving the city from British invasion.

Because of the Louisiana Purchase in 1803, New Orleans became part of the United States. The many French and Spanish residents of New Orleans had to accept a new and, to them, foreign government. In fact, most people in New Orleans did not even speak English. They resented these upstart Americans who were imposing new laws on them.

TURNABOUT'S FAIR PLAY

Jean Lafitte was a rebel at heart. He enjoyed breaking many of the new American laws. He and his Baratarians kept smuggling in illegal goods. They held "auctions" at secret locations in the swamps of Barataria, including "The Temple" and Cat Island. Many New Orleans citizens came out for the bargains. The American officials tried to put a stop to these "sales" without success. Exasperated, the American governor of Louisiana, Mr. William Claiborne, offered a reward of $500 to anyone delivering Jean Lafitte to the sheriff. Jean was in New Orleans the day the wanted posters went up. Insulted by the low amount of the reward, Lafitte paid a printer to make new posters. Late that night, he went about putting up his posters all over New Orleans, offering $1,000 reward to whoever captured the governor and brought him to Cat Island. The posters were signed "Lafitte." In small print at the bottom, it said he was "only jesting & desired that no one would do violence to his Excellency." The governor, however, did not find it very funny.

Governor Claiborne soon had his revenge. The American government was making some headway in stopping the Lafittes. Officials had raided the Lafittes' warehouses. Their property and ships were confiscated. Jean was being sued over smuggling charges. Pierre had been jailed for awhile. Several of the Baratarians were also arrested, including Dominique Youx (one of the Lafittes' officers and possibly a cousin or a brother).

THE BRITISH MAKE AN OFFER

Then the British came to Jean with an offer. They wanted his knowledge of the swamps and bayous that guarded New Orleans' backdoor. The year was 1814, and the War of 1812 between the United States and England had been raging for a few years. The British thought if they took New Orleans, they could take the whole of the Mississippi River. Then they could invade the American states from the west. The British knew of Jean and Pierre's problems with the Louisiana governor. They thought Jean would be willing to assist them, especially if they promised many rich rewards.

Even after all Governor Claiborne had done, Jean still believed in the United States. He believed in the freedoms promised by the Constitution. Instead of accepting the British offer, he went to the Americans. He convinced the newly arrived General Andrew Jackson of their willingness and ability to help. Despite recent raids by the Americans, the Lafittes had a hidden supply of gunflints and weapons (both sorely needed by the Americans). Jean offered these to Jackson. The Lafittes also had many men to contribute. Jackson accepted the offer. A pardon was promised to the Lafittes and to any of their men willing to fight.

Jean Lafitte meets with Governor Claiborne and General Jackson.

DEFENDING NEW ORLEANS

The defense of New Orleans began on December 23, 1814, with the "pirates" of Barataria helping from the start. It all ended on January 8, 1815, after an hour-and-a-half struggle called the Battle of New Orleans.

Lafitte and his men contributed greatly to the American success. Baratarians were manning many of the American cannons. They were brilliantly led by Dominique Youx. The British, who wore bright red coats and marched in orderly fashion, suffered losses of more than two thousand killed and wounded. Only eight Americans were killed and thirteen wounded.

In thanks, President Madison granted a full pardon to all the Baratarians. The Lafittes were treated as national heroes. When a victory ball was held for Jackson's officers, the Lafittes were invited. Still, Governor Claiborne would not allow the Lafittes to return to Barataria. The Lafittes were never able to recover their confiscated property or get back for damages by the Louisiana government. Jean eventually got some of his ships back, but only by purchasing them when they were sold at auction by the government.

A NEW BARATARIA

Soured on New Orleans, Jean and Pierre moved to the island of Galveston, off the coast of Texas (then in Mexican hands). They built a village called Campeachy. Others joined them at this new base, including many former Baratarians. From 1817 to 1821, the Lafittes used Galveston as their headquarters. Their ships flew the flags of countries in revolt against Spain. They claimed they only attacked Spanish vessels, but American ships were also being attacked. Jean was blamed for it. When a U.S. man-of-war ship came to Galveston, Jean found out that some of his men had acted against his orders. He quickly hanged the offenders from his men. The satisfied Americans left.

In 1821, when American ships returned claiming new charges against the Galveston pirates, the Lafittes decided it was time to go. They burned all the buildings of Campeachy. When the Americans came ashore, they saw that everyone had left. What happened to the Lafittes after that is shrouded in mystery. There are some clues they worked for Cuba as spies for awhile. Some say they settled in the Yucatan, and there is some evidence that Pierre died in a village there. Among the various stories of how Jean and Pierre met their deaths, it is hard to know the truth.

It was never clearly proven if either of the Lafittes were pirates, but they did have many shady business dealings. They enjoyed playing fast and loose with the law. It does seem very likely some of their lieutenants committed acts of piracy. The Lafittes were definitely smugglers and were the "godfathers" of New Orleans. They may have been the first American crime bosses, but they did care about the welfare of the young United States. If Governor Claiborne hadn't been so hard on them, they might have stayed in New Orleans and become more respectable businessmen. Nevertheless, New Orleans and the United States owe a lot to the Lafittes.

Real Pirate History to Visit:
Chalmette Battlefield
(part of Jean Lafitte National Park and Preserve)

8606 West St. Bernard Highway, Chalmette, Louisiana

Just downriver from New Orleans is the battlefield where the final stand for New Orleans was made on January 8, 1815. In fact, every year on the weekend near January 8, the Battle of New Orleans is reenacted at the Chalmette Battlefield, complete with a unit of Baratarians manning the guns.

More info: www.nps.gov/jela/index.htm

Pirates in the Movies:
The Buccaneer (1958)

starring Yul Brynner, is loosely based on Jean Lafitte and the Battle of New Orleans. In some ways, it is rather accurate—for a Hollywood movie. Lafitte's lieutenants mentioned in the movie were all actual people: Dominique Youx, Renato Beluche, and Vincent Gambi. Dominique Youx, a crack cannoneer, was instrumental in the Battle of New Orleans. On the other hand, the movie leaves Pierre Lafitte out completely. [NOTE: There is an earlier version of this movie (1938) with Fredric March as Lafitte. If you have time, it is fun to watch both and compare.]

YA SCURVY DOG!

TALK LIKE A PIRATE

Pirates had a rich vocabulary. They combined the nautical lingo of sailors with their own specialized cutthroat phrases. Their way of talking was unique to their way of living. You can tell they are pirates just by listening to them talk. You can hear the lustiness and swagger in their words.

TALK LIKE A PIRATE DAY

Two buddies were playing tennis one summer day in 1995. Being a little bored, they decided to make the game more fun by talking like pirates. It was "Arrrgh" this and "Blast" that for the whole time as they hit the ball back and forth. These two guys had so much fun, they decided that people should talk like pirates more often. They invented a special holiday called "Talk Like a Pirate Day." They declared September 19 as the day to celebrate. They even gave themselves pirate names—Ol' Chumbucket and Cap'n Slappy.

Little did they know what they started. For a few years, they told friends about the holiday, and a few people joined in with them. Then in 2002, Dave Barry, a newspaper columnist and author, found out about the piratical holiday. He wrote about "Talk Like a Pirate Day" in his column, and soon the whole world knew about this new holiday.

When they started this whole thing, Cap'n Slappy and Ol' Chumbucket didn't really know much about pirates. Actually, we're still not sure they know much about pirates, but that hasn't stopped them from writing several books about the fun you can have just talking and acting like a bunch of scurvy pirates.

To learn more about Talk Like a Pirate Day, the Pirate Guys, and what people are doing to celebrate, visit www.talklikeapirate.com.

Should you ever find yourselves at a loss for words, we give you . . .

THE PIRATE INSULT KIT

Buccaneers, privateers, and sailors in general were known for their lusty oaths and colorful, spicy use of the language. To help you in the use of creative and salty mockery and ridicule, use the lists on page 97. These are all words that were commonly used during the 1600s or earlier.

It's great when you can insult someone and they don't even know what you are saying! But even though they don't know what it means, it sure sounds bad.

Simply combine at least one selection (you can use more) from each of the three columns below. Examples:

Bilious crab-brained plague-rat
Horrid, ship-sinking mermaid
Cretinous, rum-sodden, grease-bellied tavern-scum

You might try mixing and matching some of the hyphenated words for extra vocabulary. Let the list inspire you to greater heights of disdain.

Brief definitions are given for those words not easily found in a modern dictionary.

GROUP 1

artless
bilious
blasted
bogstuff
  (excrement)
bootless
cockered
  (pampered)
craven
cretinous
cupshot (drunk)
currish
dankish (moist)
droning
dunderpate (oaf)
errant
fawning
fetid
fobbing (deceiving)
frothy (trifling)
froward
gleeking (jibing)
gorbellied
  (big belly)
gouty (diseased)
hapless (luckless)
horrid
impertinent
keelhauled
lubberly (oafish)
loggerheaded
lumpish (oafish)
malapert
  (rude, saucy)
mammering
  (stuttering)
mangled
mewling
paunchy
pribbling
  (quibbling)
puling
puking
putrid
rancid
rank
recreant
  (cowardly)
reeky
salty
saucy
scummy
scurrilous
scurvy
seasick
slimey
slovenly
spongy
surly
toadying
tottering
unmuzzled
venomed
vile
villainous
vomitous
wayward
weasely
weedy
weevily
yeasty
  (trifling)

GROUP 2

barnacle-encrusted
bat-fowling
beef-witted
bilge-lickin'
bilge-watered
biscuit-eatin'
black-mouthed
  (slandering)
blood-poisoned
blue-blooded
boil-brained
bold-beating
  (blustering)
bottle-pated
  (oafish)
brandy-faced
  (red faced)
bum-basted
  (beaten)
canker-ridden
chamberpot-lickin'
chum-'eatin'
clapper-clawed
  (thrashed)
clay-brained
  (stupid)
cony-catching
  (cheat)
crab-brained
dizzy-eyed
doghearted
dread-bolted
fat-kidneyed
flap-mouthed
fly-bitten
fool-born
grease-bellied
guts-griping
half-witted
high-stomached
  (haughty)
hump-backed
ill-favored
ill-nurtured
lack-witted
land-loving
light-fingered
lily-livered
lop-sided
milk-livered
maggot-infested
maggot-ridden
motley-minded
onion-eyed
plume-plucked
  (humbled)
pus-festering
rough-hewn
rum-fogged
rum-sodden
scum-spewing
scurvy-laden
sheep-hearted
slow-witted
ship-sinking (bad
  luck bringing)
sponge-spined
squid-suckin'
tickle-brained
toad-spotted
wall-eyed
weather-bitten

GROUP 3

addle (putrid urine)
addle-pate (oaf)
barnacle
bilge-rat
bilge-slop
blackguard
black-pot
  (drunkard)
blowfish
burble (pimple)
caitiff (coward)
canker-blossom
carbuncle-face
catch-fart
  (a servant who
  follows his mas-
  ter very closely)
chamberpot
churlish (oafish)
dinchpoop (dunce)
coistrell (rascal)
cormorant
  (glutton)
coxcomb (fool)
cozener (con artist)
craddon (coward)
fart-licker
foot-licker
fustilarian (scamp)
grease-boy
gudgeon
  (easy victim)
gutter-snipe
jackanapes (fool)
jelly-fish
jolthead
Jonas (bad luck)
lickspittle
lout
maggot-meat
malt-worm
measle
mermaid
  (bad luck)
milk-sop
minnow
  (easy victim)
miscreant
moldwarp
  (mole, spy)
pantaloon
  (old man)
peacock
plague-rat
poltroon (coward)
pumpion
  (pumpkin)
puttock (buzzard)
recreant (coward)
sea-cow
sea-dog
sea-slug
sea-snake
swab-stick
tavern-scum
toredo worm
tosspot
  (drunkard)
varlot
vassal
wharf-scum
whey-face

(97)

Aliases &
Nom de Guerres:
Pirate Names

*P*irates often got their nicknames and aliases from something they did, or from their appearance. Blackbeard, of course, had a big black beard. Olivier La Bouche was known as "The Buzzard," perhaps because he looted dead bodies.

For your pirate persona, you might pick a nickname from something special about your pirate. This may take a little time as you decide on your pirate's background. However, if you and your friends need a quick way of picking out nicknames, perhaps for a pirate party, you can create a three-column chart. In the first column, list descriptive words such as Red, Black, Nasty, Tall, Mad, One-Eye, Smilin', Fancy, Pegleg, Scruffy, etc. In the second column, give names such as Jack, Rita, Ted, Rosie, Francois, Dan, Bart, Meg, Juan, Thomas, Billy, Annie, Israel, Francois, Rock, Pierre, Roger, Grace, Mary, etc. The third column provides a fake title such as "the Terrible," "the Forgetful," "the Hook," "the Mighty," "the Gruesome," etc. Choose one name from each column, or you could make it a chance game—throwing darts or tossing coins on the chart. Of course, if you come up with "Slack-jawed Thomas the Forgetful," just throw the darts again. You could set a limit on how many times you can throw, possibly three.

FINDING YER INNER PIRATE

Have you ever wanted to become someone else? Someone completely different—maybe a pirate like Long John Silver, Captain Jack Sparrow, or Anne Bonny?

Well, now you're learning how to TALK like a pirate, but it's also time to learn how to become the pirate you always wanted to be. This is where a little acting and imagination comes in. And a lot of fun!

You can abandon your regular self and become someone with a very different life. You don't have to figure out everything about your pirate character or persona right away. You can create him or her slowly over time. And don't worry if you don't get everything right the first time. You can always change anything about your character you don't like or start over with a whole new persona.

You can "put on" and "take off" this persona like a set of clothes. In fact, when you put on your pirate costume, it is the perfect time to put on your persona too.

WHO AM I?

Here are some basic questions that will help you create your pirate. As you decide who your pirate is, write your pirate's biography (life story). You might also draw pictures to go with your answers. Draw what you and your fellow crewmates look like. If you cannot come up with the answer for something right away, that's okay. It may come to you later. Remember, any part of your story can be changed later on. Nothing is set in stone.

WHAT IS MY NAME?

What is my nickname or alias? Do I have more than one nickname or alias? (See the previous section on page 98. You might want to wait until you answer some of the questions below, and then maybe a name will come easily to you.)

WHAT DO I LOOK LIKE?

Am I tall/short? What color are my hair and eyes? Do I walk with a limp or have a squinty eye? Do I have any scars? How did I get them? (See page 73 for how to create scars.)

FINDING YER INNER PIRATE

(*Continued*)

HOW DO I DRESS?

What do I wear? Are my clothes clean or neat (not likely)? Dirty and torn?

Do I have rich clothes (perhaps stolen)? Or just basic sailor clothes? If you don't have fancy pirate clothes yet, then it will be easier to start at the bottom as a basic sailor (see pages 68–70 to make your own Basic Sailor costume). You can always get promoted to captain later on.

WHEN DO I LIVE?

Am I from the 1580s (the time of Sir Francis Drake, Sir Walter Raleigh, and the Sea Dogs), the 1660s (the time of Henry Morgan, Port Royal, Tortuga, and the buccaneers), the 1710s (the era of Blackbeard, Sam Bellamy, and the Golden Age of Pirates), or the 1810s (when Jean Lafitte and the Baratarians ruled the Gulf of Mexico)? Or some other time period?

WHERE DID I COME FROM?

What country was I born in? Am I French, English, Spanish, Irish, Scottish, etc.? Am I from the American colonies? Or a Spanish colony? (If you know another language, even if just a little, it could be fun to be a character from that country.) What town/city did I come from? What did I do before becoming a pirate?

WHO IS MY FAMILY?

Are they rich or poor? Are they sailors, farmers, city people, merchants, gypsies, or members of a wandering acting troupe?

HOW DID I BECOME A PIRATE? WHY?

Did pirates capture the ship I was on and invite me to join? Did I hear about a pirate crew forming up to go "on the account"? Did I stow away on a ship, not realizing it was a pirate ship?

WHERE AM I NOW?

What country? Am I part of a ship's crew? Do I live on a ship? What is my ship's name? What kind of ship is she? Draw a picture of your pirate ship. What is my captain's name? What is my job on the ship? Who are some of my crewmates? (Maybe some of your friends have also created pirate personas and you can be on the same crew.)

If I don't live on a ship, do I live in town? In the jungle? On a deserted island?

DO I HAVE ANY SKILLS?

Can I read and write? Can I do a little "figuring" (adding and subtracting)? Did I go to school? Do I know how to fight? What weapons do I use? Do I sing or play an instrument? Are there any special things I can do?

HOW DO I TALK?

Is my voice rough and gravelly? Low and mysterious? Big and booming? Do I lisp, mumble, or slur my words? Do I have an accent?

WHAT ARE SOME OF THE THINGS I HAVE DONE?

Have I ever stolen anything or rescued anyone? Have I been in battle? Was I at the sack of Panama with Captain Henry Morgan?

WHAT PLACES HAVE I BEEN?

Have I sailed around the world? Or maybe I've never even crossed the equator.

Perhaps my origins were humble. I was a poor peasant, stable boy, or overworked apprentice who wanted to go to sea to seek his fortune. Could I be the son or daughter of a rich merchant or nobleman who ran off to sea in search of adventure?

If I am a girl, did I disguise myself as a boy so I could enlist as a sailor aboard a merchant ship? It would be easy to become a pirate from there. Pirates were always looking to recruit more sailors.

Maybe I was in the army. Did the war end and I had no job to go back to? Or did I run away and become a deserter? Was I a pickpocket or thief who was caught and sentenced to be an indentured servant in the Americas? Did I later escape and run away when my master treated me badly?

LETTING YOUR STORY GROW

It's all right to be a little mysterious at first or not to know the answers to all the questions above. It will come to you bit by bit. It might change a little or a lot, and that's okay. The simpler your story, the easier it is to remember it.

The more you read about pirates and learn about pirate history, the more your pirate persona will grow too.

SOUNDING LIKE A PIRATE

Develop your "pirate voice." Memorize and practice some of the pirate talk in this chapter, then try telling a short story in your pirate voice.

Do you have an accent or dialect? Listen to characters with that accent and try to say things the way they do. One way to learn accents is to watch pirate movies. Imitate a character that talks as your pirate would talk. Here are some movies and specific characters to listen to for practicing accents:

FINDING YER INNER PIRATE

(Continued)

ENGLISH ACCENT
Treasure Island (1950), especially Long John Silver (Robert Newton). *The Scarecrow of Romney Marsh* (1963), Dr. Christopher Syn (Patrick McGoohan). *Peter Pan* (2003), Captain Hook (Jason Isaacs).

IRISH ACCENT
Swashbuckler (1976), specifically Captain "Red" Ned Lynch (Robert Shaw). *The Black Swan* (1942), Tommy Blue (Thomas Mitchell). *Darby O'Gill and the Little People* (1959). Not a pirate movie, but it does include a lot of Irish accents.

SCOTTISH ACCENT
Muppet Treasure Island (1996), Billy Bones (Billy Connolly).

FRENCH ACCENT
The Buccaneer (1958), Dominique Youx (Charles Boyer) along with other characters. *Captain Blood* (1935), Le Vasseur (Basil Rathbone).

SPANISH ACCENT
The Princess Bride (1987), Inigo Montoya (Mandy Patinkin).

BECOME YOUR PIRATE

Now here's the fun part: becoming your pirate. Practice at home first, in your bedroom or backyard or in front of the mirror. Then try your character on your friends or your family (you might let your parents know what you are doing before your mom gets upset when you call her a "saucy lass"). Can you "stay in character" all through dinner? Talk with your family and answer questions as your pirate would?

You probably don't want to bring your pirate character to school though. He or she could get you in trouble with your teachers.

After you've practiced a bit at home, you might go to a party (especially a pirate party) as your pirate. Or show up at a pirate festival. You will probably find being dressed as your pirate makes it easier to "be" your pirate. Try to be your pirate for the whole time. Talk and interact with people as your pirate would. Don't talk about modern things like TV, movies, computers, or cars. Don't talk on your cell phone. Do the things your pirate would do (within reason—no stealing, killing, or marooning allowed).

If you believe you ARE your pirate, then everyone else will believe in your pirate, too.

PIRATES' DICTIONARY

Ahoy: A call used in hailing, as in "Ship ahoy!"

Armada: Spanish term for a fleet of warships.

Articles: A contract or treaty among the crew of a ship, or of several ships working together, drawn up and signed before going out on the account.

Avast!: Stop! Hold! Cease! Stay! It means to immediately stop whatever you are doing.

Batten down the hatches: Hatches were openings in the deck to cargo holds below. In rough weather, tarpaulins (tarred cloths; also called tarps) were stretched over these openings, and small pieces of wood (battens) were wedged in along the sides to keep them in place.

Belay (or "Belay that"): To stop whatever you are doing. To belay a line means to wrap the loose end about a pin in the railing.

Belly timber: Food, especially meat.

Bilged upon her anchor: When a ship's anchor pierces its own hull.

Careenage: A place for careening a ship, usually a sheltered bay or cove, to make repairs.

Clap in irons: To chain someone up.

Crimp: Someone who swindles or kidnaps seamen.

Davy Jones' Locker: Essentially, the bottom of the sea. Davy Jones was an evil spirit living in the sea. He received dead sailors in his "locker."

Doubloon: A gold Spanish coin.

Execution Dock: The place where pirate hangings usually took place in London. It was on the banks of the Thames River, near the Tower of London.

Fireship: A special vessel loaded with explosives and flammable goods, ignited, and set adrift towards the enemy.

Flota: Fleet (in Spanish); usually refers to the Silver Fleet that annually returned to Spain with acquired treasure from the New World.

Flotilla: A small fleet.

From the sea: The answer a pirate ship in open waters would give when asked where they come from.

Gibbet: a wooden scaffolding from which bodies of executed criminals were displayed as a warning to others.

Handsomely: Done carefully, smartly.

Jack: A small flag, usually flown at a ship's bow, to show nationality or act as a signal.

Kill Devil: A favorite pirate name for rum.

Land ho!: Land has been sighted (can also be "Ship ho!"). This is the report from the lookout. From the deck, he is asked "Where away?" and he will then give direction: "Dead ahead," "On the starboard bow," etc.

Letters of marque: A commission, usually granted by the government, to the commander of a merchant ship or privateer allowing him to cruise against and make prizes of enemy ships and vessels. In return, he was expected to return a set portion of any prizes to the crown.

Lubber (landlubber): An awkward, clumsy oaf, or a green, not-too-bright sailor.

Man-of-war: A warship.

Mate: A companion, fellow worker. Derived from a word meaning "meat," it originally referred to those who shared food. Later, it became the title of an officer, the one who saw that the captain's orders were carried out.

No prey, no pay: Pirate version of the phrase "No purchase, no pay" (see *Purchase*).

No quarter given: No mercy (quarter) is to be shown, no prisoners will be taken. A red flag meant no quarter given and was intended to strike terror into the hearts of the pirates' victims.

On the account: A term for going out a-pirating. Actually, it originally meant that no wages were to be paid, and there would be no compensation until plunder was taken. Originated with the privateers.

Pieces of eight: A Spanish coin of silver. It was worth eight reales.

Purchase: Payment in the form of loot, as in the saying "No purchase, no pay," used by the privateers.

Prize: Usually refers to a captured ship. If a pirate calls a lady this, it is to be sure that he has been checkin' her out.

Punishment of Moses: A flogging of "Forty stripes, less one, on the bare back," or thirty-nine lashes.

Quarter: Means that mercy will be shown if the pirate's victim surrenders. It meant the sparing of lives and possibly freedom (or ransom) after the pirate was through taking what he wanted. A black flag (Jolly Roger) meant that quarter would be offered.

Road: A partly sheltered place to anchor.

Salmagundi: (Various spellings.) A favorite meal of the buccaneers; basically a stew of anything at hand, including anchovies, hard-boiled eggs, and limes.

Scurvy: As an adjective, it means sorry, contemptible, good for nothing. As a noun, it was the name for a disease caused by the lack of fresh food in a sailor's diet.

Sea artists: Specialists aboard ship, such as navigators, sailing masters, carpenters, surgeons, and gunners.

Shantyman: A crewmember who sings and composes songs (often rude) for the enjoyment of his mates.

Shiver me timbers: (Fictional in origin.) A phrase of surprise or shock. It refers to the effect of a cannonball on the oak timbers of the ship. A cannonball blast would send showers of large splinters (6 inches or longer), which would be more deadly than the cannonball itself (especially due to death by infection). The splinters are called shivers.

Sloop: The favorite pirate vessel of the early 1700s. It had a bowsprit (a pole like a mast sticking out straight in front) almost as long as the rest of the ship. With this bowsprit, a sloop could carry a vast spread of canvas. It could go fast and sail in shallow water. It was great for quick hit-and-run attacks.

Spanish Main: Central American and northern South American coast held by the Spanish and often raided by buccaneers.

Strike the colors: To bring down a ship's flag as a sign of surrender.

Swag: Loot, plunder, stolen goods.

The Sweet Trade: Another term for piracy, buccaneering.

Swivel: Short for "swivel gun." A gun mounted usually on the ship's railing, on a pivot, so it can be swung from side to side.

Tar: A sailor. It comes from the use of tar to saturate the sailors' overclothes to make them water resistant. Also, tar from the lines stained their hands and clothes.

Vice-Admiralty Courts: Courts set up by the British government to hear and try maritime offenses.

Watch: On a regular ship, the crew is divided into two watches (like teams), one of which sails while the other is sleeping or resting. Each period of duty (which generally lasts four hours) is also called a watch. Pirate ships might or might not have used this system of watches. [Not to be confused with a timepiece].

Weigh (as in "weigh anchor"): To raise a vessel's anchor prior to departure.

BUT I WANNA SIGN THE ARTICLES!

THE BOY WHO HAD TO BE A PIRATE

John King was just an ordinary boy living with his mother until a fateful event occurred that would change his life forever . . .

At least his life was ordinary until he met the charismatic pirate captain Samuel "Black Sam" Bellamy. John was traveling with his mother from the island of Jamaica to another British colony on Antigua aboard the sloop *Bonetta*.

The voyage was uneventful until November 9, 1716. According to the captain's log, that was the day they were attacked and captured by Samuel Bellamy and his crew of pirates. Bellamy tied his sloop, the *Marianne*, alongside the *Bonetta* and spent fifteen days thoroughly ransacking the vessel. The passengers aboard the *Bonetta* may have been horrified by their ordeal, but young John King was thrilled. He was fascinated by the colorful pirates and especially by their charismatic leader. After some of the *Bonetta's* crew decided to join the pirates, John was determined to become a pirate himself.

The pirates were probably amused by the young boy who followed them around and insisted that he wanted to be a pirate, too! But they never took him seriously until one day he demanded that Captain Bellamy let him join his pirate crew. Bellamy was reluctant to let such a young boy (John was reported to be between 8 and 11 years old at the time) join his crew. But John declared that he would kill himself if anybody tried to stop him. When his mother protested and tried to interfere, he threatened her as well.

Bellamy must have admired the boy's spirit and show of defiance. He changed his mind and decided to let the boy aboard the *Marianne*. John made history that day, becoming one of the youngest boys ever known to have signed the articles and joined a pirate crew.

But his career as a pirate was short-lived. He lasted less than three months before he met his end. A few months after taking John aboard, Captain Bellamy captured the slave ship *Whydah* and transferred himself and part of his crew aboard, including John King. After taking several prizes, Bellamy decided it was time to head home. Bellamy's small pirate fleet headed north for Maine, but Bellamy never made it. The *Whydah* was wrecked off the coast of Cape Cod when she violently ran aground during a storm. As the *Whydah* capsized, canons and other articles broke loose and crashed across the deck. John was hurled so violently across the deck that his leg bone was impaled in a pewter teapot. Then one of the ship's cannon came crashing down upon him. It was the end.

How do we know this, you might ask? Because they found John's leg bone inside his silk stocking with his shoe. It was concreted together with the teapot under that same cannon. It must have been a horrible way to die. Sometimes, it just doesn't pay to defy your mother.

NOTORIOUS LADIES OF THE SEA

Not all pirates were men and boys. Some were women, and even a few were teenage girls. We know about ten to twenty female pirates, depending on how you define them (some might be considered privateers or smugglers instead, and a couple might be hoaxes). Who knows how many more women pirates were disguised as men and never discovered or how many women pirates were lost in history? Let's take a look at the ones we know about.

ALFHILD
(ALSO RECORDED AS ALWILDA, ALVIDA, OR ALTIDA)

Alfhild was a Scandinavian princess who some say lived around 450 CE while others say it was after 850 CE. The Danish historian Saxo Grammaticus told her story, though it's not certain if she truly existed. According to Grammaticus, she was a princess who decided to became a pirate rather than marry Prince Alf of Denmark against her will. She first commanded an all-female crew, and then was later elected by a male crew to be their leader. Meanwhile, Alf had gone in his ship to look for her. In a true fairy-tale ending, Alf's ship and her ship battled at sea. He won the battle, and they got married. She gave up piracy to stay home and give birth to a daughter. Whether or not she was happy with this arrangement, the stories don't say.

BONNY, ANNE

Anne was the daughter of a lawyer who left Ireland to settle in South Carolina. Anne grew up willful and wild, and later married the sailor James Bonny against her father's wishes. James started hanging out with pirates, which is when Anne met the notorious "Calico Jack," aka Captain John Rackham (see below). She joined Jack's crew disguised as a man. Mary Read later joined the crew (see Read, Mary on page 111). In 1720, they were captured and brought to trial. The male members of the crew were hanged. Anne and Mary "pleaded their bellies" because they were pregnant. A pregnant woman was not hanged until after her baby was born. It's unknown what happened to Anne after the trial. Some people think her rich father paid the officials to let her go free.

Name: John Rackham

Alias: Calico Jack

Dates: active as a pirate as early as 1718; hanged in 1720

Country: England

Ship: *William*

Flag: Rackham's flag was said to be a grinning skull above a pair of crossed cutlasses. It was "pirated" by Disney as the flag of the *Black Pearl* in the *Pirates of the Caribbean* films. There are no eyewitness accounts of which flag Rackham flew, so we can't say for sure this design was his.

Best known for: John Rackham was known by the nickname "Calico Jack" because of the colorful calico outfits he wore. He caused a sensation after his capture when it was revealed that two of his crew were actually women pirates. Anne Bonny and Mary Read had fought fiercely to protect their ship. The men had been too drunk to fight and had cowered belowdeck.

BURN, FLORA

A female privateer, one of the thirty-five-member crew of the privateer *Revenge* sailing off the American coast in 1741. Very little is know about her other than her name is on the ship's crew list.

CHENG I SAO (OR ZHENG YI SAO OR CHING, MRS.)

She controlled the largest band of pirates ever! She was the wife of the leader of a Chinese pirate fleet in the early 1800s. Her name translates to simply mean "wife of Cheng I." Her personal name was Shih Hsiang-ku, and she was said to be a great beauty. When Cheng I died suddenly in 1807, she took over leadership of the fleet and made it even stronger. Cheng I Sao became so powerful that she was able to dictate the terms of her own amnesty with the Chinese government. She then retired and set up a gambling house in Canton.

LAI CHOI SAN

Like Mrs. Ching, Lai Choi San controlled a fleet of Chinese junks in the South China Seas. She was active in the 1920s and '30s. Her story is told by only one person: American reporter Aleko Lilius. It has not been confirmed by other sources. Some believe her to be fictional or a greatly exaggerated truth. Her story, however, was the basis for The Dragon Lady, the cold-hearted arch-villainess in "Terry and the Pirates," a newspaper comic strip of the 1930s and 1940s.

GRANUAILE
(GRANIA NY MAILLE OR GRACE O'MALLEY)

Granuaile was a pirate and clan leader on the western Irish coast. She lived around 1530–1603 CE. Her proper name was Grania ny Maille. Granuaile is a nickname meaning "The Bald One," most likely because she cut her hair short. Grace O'Malley is just an English version of her name. Many legends have grown up around her, so it is hard to sort out the truth, but she definitely existed. She lived at about the same time as Queen Elizabeth I of England. During this time, England was invading Ireland, and Grania, with her fleet of pirates, became a problem for the queen. Grania met with Elizabeth to sort things out. The two women communicated in Latin, because Granuaile did not speak English and Elizabeth did not speak Irish. They came to an agreement, and Elizabeth gave Grania a letter of marque. Grania lived a very long life and died the same year as Queen Elizabeth. In 2007, there was a Broadway musical production based on Grania's life, called *The Pirate Queen.*

KILLIGREW, LADY MARY

Elizabethan-era pirate who was active in the mid 1500s. She was perhaps the wife or the mother of Sir John Killigrew (history isn't always clear on details like this because a father and son often shared the same name). He was the head of a large smuggling operation in Falmouth Harbor, Cornwall (the southwest corner of England). In 1577, John was accused of buying stolen French wines from a pirate. He settled the matter by paying the real owners for the wine. Lady Killigrew is famous for leading an attack on a Spanish (some say German) cargo ship that took shelter in their harbor in the winter of 1580–81. She had heard there was a hoard of pieces of eight aboard. She and two of the men with her were arrested. The two men were hanged, but she was reprieved at the last minute. There is some confusion if Sir John paid bribes to free her or if Queen Elizabeth reprieved Lady Killigrew. Also, some stories say Lady Killigrew ordered the raid but did not participate herself. So it is unclear if Lady Killigrew is actually a pirate or not.

THE MAID ON THE SHORE

(Traditional Ballad)

There is a young maiden, she lives all alone,
She lives all alone on the shore-o
There's nothing she can find to comfort her mind.
But to roam all alone on the shore, shore, shore,
But to roam all alone on the shore.

'Twas of the young Captain who sailed the salt sea
Let the wind blow high, blow low
"I will die, I will die" the young Captain did cry
"If I don't have that maid on the shore, shore, shore,
If I don't have that maid on the shore."

"I have lots of silver, I have lots of gold
I have lots of costly ware-o
I'll divide, I'll divide with my jolly ship's crew
If they row me that maid on the shore, shore, shore,
If they row me that maid on the shore."

After much persuasion, they got her aboard
Let the wind blow high, blow low
They replaced her away in his cabin below
"Here's adieu to all sorrow and care, care, care,
Here's adieu to all sorrow and care."

READ, MARY

Immediately after her birth in England, Mary's mother dressed her as a boy to fool her mother-in-law, who thought the baby was a boy. Mary was used to acting and dressing as a boy, so when she grew up, she joined the army. She kept her secret from everyone until she fell in love with her tent mate. She told him she was a woman, and he fell in love with her too. They left the army and bought a tavern in Flanders (presently in the Netherlands). Mary was happy until one day her husband died. She then put on her men's clothes again and went to sea as a sailor, perhaps using the name Mark Read. Pirates captured her ship, and she was invited to become a pirate with Calico Jack's crew, where she met Anne Bonny. Mary told Anne her secret and soon the whole crew knew. When the crew was captured in 1720, the men were hanged, but since she was pregnant (like Anne), she was held in jail until her baby was born. In April 1721, she died while still in jail, perhaps of a fever or of problems giving birth. (See Bonny, Anne on page 108.)

They replaced her away in his cabin below
Let the wind blow high, blow low
She's so pretty and neat, she's so sweet and complete
She's sung Captain and sailors to sleep, sleep, sleep,
She's sung Captain and sailors to sleep.

Then she robbed him of silver, she robbed him of gold
She robbed him of costly ware-o
Then took his broadsword instead of an oar
And paddled her way to the shore, shore, shore,
And paddled her way to the shore.

"Me men must be crazy, me men must be mad
Me men must be deep in despair-o
For to let you away from my cabin so gay
And to paddle your way to the shore, shore, shore,
And to paddle your way to the shore."

"Your men was not crazy, your men was not mad
Your men was not deep in despair-o
I deluded your sailors as well as yourself
I'm a maiden again on the shore, shore, shore,
I'm a maiden again on the shore."

(repeat 1st verse)

TALBOT, MARY ANNE

According to her autobiography, Mary Anne was the daughter of Lord Talbot, but he was not married to her mother. As a teenager, her guardian, Captain Essex Bowen, dressed her up as a footboy, called her "John Taylor," and forced her to go with him to the Caribbean. He later made her a drummer boy in his regiment. She was able to escape only after his death in 1783. Trying to return home to England, she signed aboard a ship as a sailor. Too late, she found out it was a privateer. She next changed ships to the *Brunswick* and became the captain's cabin boy. She later retired and wrote her story. She died in 1808 at the young age of thirty, due to the many battle wounds that afflicted her. She had never properly healed from a musket ball wound in her left thigh and a shattered kneecap. She certainly did exist, but whether all of her story is true or not, we don't know.

UNKNOWN PRIVATEER CAPTAIN

In 1805, an American who was held prisoner in Cuba reported on a French privateer vessel, *La Baugourt*. He said the ship had a crew of one hundred, "commanded by a woman." This is about all that is known of this unnamed captain.

WALL, RACHEL

Rachel's husband, George Wall, served aboard an American privateer during the American Revolution. They married after the war and together stole a sloop in Essex County, Massachusetts. With a pirate crew of four, they would pose as a fishing family. After big storms, they fooled other ships by pretending to be sinking. Rachel stood on the deck, screaming for help, while the others hid. When a ship came to help them, they murdered the would-be rescuers, then robbed the vessel and sank it. No one was the wiser. In 1782, a hurricane washed George and another crewmember overboard and they drowned. Rachel's screams for help were real this time. After this close call, Rachel retired from piracy and got a job as a maid. She was later hanged in 1789 for a murder she did not commit. The night before her death, she confessed to all the piracies she had committed. She hoped her death would be a warning to young women to stay away from bad people. Rachel Wall was the last woman to be hanged in the state of Massachusetts.

"X" MARKS THE SPOT

There are very few cases of pirates burying treasure, and there were even fewer authentic pirate treasure maps. Pirates usually spent their plunder as fast as they could once they made it back to port. So where did we get the idea of Xs on maps indicating treasure?

MAKING ANTIQUE PAPER FOR MAPS, MESSAGES, AND MORE!

Even though we know there were few, if any, pirate treasure maps, they are still fun to make. For a "real" looking treasure map, you need paper that looks really old, like it's been around for a few hundred years.

It's not easy to buy this kind of paper. You can get "parchment" paper from office supply stores, but it's nothing like the real thing. It looks phony. REAL parchment is yellowed, mottled in places, and cracked along the edges. REAL parchment is made from sheepskin! That's why a slang term for a diploma is a "sheepskin." Though real parchment is from a sheep, after you make your paper, you will be able to claim "No Sheep Have Been Harmed in the Making of This Parchment."

You will need:

† paper (see below for details)
† bucket
† tea, coffee, and/or brown acrylic paint

PAPER: You can use plain typing paper, but it is nice to get paper that is bigger. Try to get a larger piece, perhaps white butcher wrapping paper. You can also use brown craft paper or even brown paper bags (try to find a bag with no writing on it, or just use the part of the bag that is blank).

Trim your paper to the size you want it. Don't use scissors. Straight, even edges just don't look right. Instead, fold the paper where you would cut it. Fold it over one way, then back the other. Do this a few times. Then use a damp sponge to get the folded edge wet. You will then tear the paper apart. The paper should tear very easily along the dampened edge. Just tear very slowly, and if other rips start, go slower. You can also use the edge of a kitchen counter or table to tear along. Torn edges have little fibers sticking out and a few little cracks, and look much more like the edges of old paper.

Fold the paper as if you were making it small enough to fit into an envelope. Open it and, at the folds, fold it back the other way. Do this over and over until it looks like someone has kept it folded in his or her vest pocket for years but brings it out now and then to look at it.

Then wad your paper up into a ball and flatten it out again. Do this a few times. The idea is to make your paper look like a long-lost document that has been worn and stained by neglect and time.

In a small bucket, mix some brownish water using any of a number of things (tea, coffee, brown acrylic paints, etc.). Do not make your stain too strong or it will make your paper too dark. Now, put your crumpled paper into the brownish water, squeezing and releasing the paper like a sponge until the water has worked completely into the paper.

For the last step, lay the paper out flat in the sun to dry and get crisp (be careful if there is any wind so it doesn't get blown all over the yard). You've now got some old-looking paper, perfect for your treasure map creation. This type of paper is also great for authentic-looking invitations, signs, etc.

The author Robert Louis Stevenson was very close to his young stepson Lloyd. One rainy afternoon in 1883, Lloyd was amusing himself with his paints. He later recalled:

> . . . busy with a box of paints I happened to be tinting a map of an island I had drawn. Stevenson came in as I was finishing it, and with his affectionate interest in everything I was doing, leaned over my shoulder, and was soon elaborating the map and naming it. I shall never forget the thrill of Skeleton Island, Spyglass Hill, nor the heart-stirring climax of the three red crosses! And the greater climax still when he wrote down the words "Treasure Island" at the top right-hand corner! And he seemed to know so much about it too—the pirates, the buried treasure, the man who had been marooned on the island. . . . "Oh, for a story about it," I exclaimed, in a heaven of enchantment.

Stevenson wrote the stories down. They became his first major success and one of his most popular books. The book was originally called *The Sea Cook*. Luckily, his editor changed it to the title we know now: *Treasure Island*.

THE MONEY PIT OF OAK ISLAND

It is not certain whether the Money Pit of Oak Island is connected with pirates or whether it contains any treasure, but it certainly has the right name. Over the years, a large fortune has been spent digging for what treasure might be there.

Oak Island is a 140-acre island just a few hundred feet from the coast of Nova Scotia, on the east coast of Canada. Today there is a land bridge connecting it with the mainland.

More than two hundred years ago, in 1795, teenager Daniel McGinnis went canoeing by himself. It was early summer. He paddled around Oak Island and tied up his canoe. He got out to explore the woods.

He found a man-made clearing. In the middle was a spot on the ground that sank down a little. It looked like what happens when you dig a hole and fill it back in. The sinkhole was about 13 feet across. Next to the sinkhole was an old oak tree. One of its branches hung over the sinkhole. Some say there was even an old tackle block dangling from this limb. Daniel immediately thought of pirates and buried loot. Stories had gone around that the island was haunted—people had seen lights on the island at night. Maybe they had seen the lanterns of the pirates burying their treasure.

Daniel rushed off and came back the next day with two friends, John Smith and Anthony Vaughn. The teenagers began digging. A couple of feet below ground level they found a layer of flat stones. Below that was the mouth of a round shaft going straight down. It had been filled back in with softer dirt. They kept digging.

The soft dirt was easy to remove. At ten feet down one of the shovels hit wood. They were thrilled. They thought they had found a wooden chest of treasure. Instead, they uncovered a platform of oak logs. The ends of the logs were securely stuck into the walls of the pit. They pulled the logs out and saw they were very rotten. The logs had been there a long time. They thought the treasure had to be just below the platform. They found nothing except a two-foot gap of air, and then more dirt. They figured if someone had gone to all this trouble, there had to be a fantastic treasure waiting below. They kept digging and digging. Day after day. Just more dirt. When the hole got to 25 feet deep, the digging got too hard. The boys realized they needed more help. They drove wooden sticks into the sides of the shaft to keep the sides from falling in. They covered the hole with trees and brush. It was the end of summer.

Right after they discovered the Money Pit, John Smith bought the parcel of land it was on. He eventually bought twenty-four acres, the whole eastern side of the island. He built a house near the pit so he could keep an eye on the treasure hole.

It was not until eight or nine years later when anyone returned to dig the hole again. This time they came with hired men and heavy equipment.

Finally, the digging had resumed. Eventually a shovel hit wood again. Everyone was excited. This was it! But no, it was ANOTHER platform of oak logs. They dug farther. The shaft just kept going. As they dug, they went through layers of various materials, including charcoal, putty, dried grass, and coconut fiber. They also found other wooden platforms, perhaps at 10-foot intervals. At 90 feet deep, they found a 3-foot by 15-inch flat stone with cryptic markings carved on it (the markings might have been added after it was found). At this point, water started seeping in. At 93 feet the water was coming in really fast. It was getting dark. Just before leaving for the night, someone probed the bottom of the pit with a long iron bar to get an idea of what was waiting next. At about 5 feet deeper, the bar struck a hard layer.

INVITE YER CREW

For your next party, rather than sending a simple announcement in an envelope, make the invitations something special with a hint of the adventure to come. You might wish to print your own invitations, using parchment paper, perhaps fashioned as a treasure map with directions to your house. Follow the techniques on page 114–115 to make your invitations look really old. You could even burn the edges of the paper (ask a parent for help on this). You can print onto the parchment paper with your computer or draw your invitations by hand. (If you plan to print onto the plain paper with your printer, do this BEFORE you put the paper through the "antiquing" process. Wrinkled-up paper will not easily go through your printer.)

FANCY SCROLL INVITATIONS

Roll up the invitations scroll-fashion and tie them up with a red, gold, or black ribbon. You might even seal them with wax. Wax and sealers are available at fancy stationery stores and some craft stores. You can get a seal with a skull-and-crossbones design or one with your initials, or use whatever design you like. Light the wax candle to drip a puddle of wax onto the edge of the rolled-up scroll, right where the ribbon crosses it. Before the wax cools too much, squish the metal seal into the wax puddle and let it sit for 10 seconds or so. When you pull the seal out of the wax, it will leave the design in the wax. (Have mom or dad help you with this part.)

DELIVERING THE SCROLLS

You can hand-deliver the scrolls or send them in mailing tubes. Better yet, send your invitations as messages in a bottle (see page 60).

Pastimes for Scurvy Dogs

OPEN THE TREASURE CHEST

For this activity, you need a "real" treasure chest with a working lock. Get several copies of the key made. Also, collect several old keys. You will need at least one for every guest. Put the keys together in a tankard or mug. Let each of your guests pick a key. Then they get a shot at opening the chest. Some pirates get a key that works, others get a key that doesn't work. Inside the chest can be treasure to pick from (items from the dollar store or Oriental Trading Company). Give an eye patch or some other consolation prize to those whose keys did not work.

That was a Saturday night, and they would not be able to resume digging until Monday. All day Sunday they were probably imagining, more so than ever, what could be in the pit. Were they finally near the bottom? Could it be Captain Kidd's buried treasure just waiting for them?

On Monday when they returned, they were shocked to find the water level had risen. The pit was filled with seawater to the 33-foot level! They started bailing with buckets. Day and night they worked with no change in water level. They brought in a pump, but it promptly broke under the task. They finally gave up.

They didn't know at the time, but no amount of pumping could lower the water. The flooding was from a booby trap! There was a side tunnel connected with an underwater opening off the coast of the island.

In 1805, a second shaft was dug 14 feet away from the first. Then they dug sideways, at the level of where the imagined treasure lay at about 100 feet. As they got within two feet of the original shaft, water broke through. Water and debris quickly filled the second shaft to the same level as the first. The workers were lucky to get out alive!

Since then, there have been many efforts to find out what is at the bottom of the Money Pit. There has been failure after failure, though many interesting discoveries have been made along the way. More flood tunnels were discovered later by other fortune-hunting teams. Millions of dollars have been spent trying to find what is in the Money Pit.

Why so much effort? Will it be worth it when someone finally gets to the bottom of all this? Who could have built such a structure? And why? Very few clues have been found: some links of chain, a pair of scissors, a stone with the date 1704, a whistle carved of bone, and a scrap of parchment.

In 1971, a group of treasure hunters made drill holes down more than 200 feet deep. At 230 feet, the shaft opened up into a cavity in the bedrock. They lowered an underwater camera into it. The treasure hunters watched the camera's image on a fuzzy television screen. At the depth of about 235 feet, they saw what looked like three sea chests guarded by a severed human hand!

Researchers have estimated the complex structure of the pit took about fifty men working for a year to finish. Some people think Captain William Kidd buried his treasure on Oak Island. But he and his crew didn't have enough time to dig this pit. Others think Blackbeard is the mysterious builder of the pit. Mysterious lights and fires were seen on the island in 1763, but that would have been too late for Kidd or Blackbeard. There are many other possible explanations for what is buried on Oak Island and who put it there. The mystery is still unsolved.

The real puzzle of the flood traps is how the builders planned to get their buried treasure back.

Excavation accidents have killed six men to date. There is a legend that the secret of the Money Pit will be found when seven fortune hunters have given their lives and all the oaks are gone from the island. Let's hope the legend is wrong and the elusive treasure can be found with no more loss of life.

Pastimes for Scurvy Dogs

TREASURE HUNT

To create a treasure hunt for you and your friends, write cryptic clues and hide them throughout your yard or in a park. If near water, put some clues in bottles dangling out in the water, tied to something on land so they won't drift away. Hang clues from trees, under rocks, in nooks and crannies. Have one clue lead to the next. Divide everyone into teams. Let them start when the ship's bell is rung. First team to solve all the clues and make it back to ring the bell wins a treasure chest of goodies.

GOLD!

I am rich Potosí
Treasure of the world
The king of all mountains
And the envy of all kings.
—Translation of the motto of the city of Potosí

The Spanish and other Europeans valued gold and silver above almost all other things. When they came to the Americas, one of the first things they asked the natives was, "Is there any gold around here?" Well, actually, they would have spoken Spanish, not English. And the natives probably didn't understand Spanish. They probably communicated with sign language, with the eager-for-riches Spanish showing the natives some gold coins or a golden cross and trying to find out if the natives had seen any of the glittery stuff.

The native peoples of America did not value gold, other than as pretty stuff to make jewelry and other things out of. They usually showed the Spanish where to find gold and silver, but often were not treated very well in return. In fact, there was a LOT of silver (and some gold) in the New World.

The Spanish really hit the jackpot in 1545. That is the year when they discovered Cerro de Potosí (also called Cerro Rico, "Rich Mountain"). In the Andean Mountains of Peru (in what is now Bolivia), they found a huge mountain with massive amounts of silver. It stood 15,381 feet high (almost a 1,000 feet taller than Mt. Whitney in California).

Pirates in the Movies: Silver Mule Train

You can see the capture of a silver mule train in *The Sea Hawk* (1940, Errol Flynn). This capture is loosely based on the silver mule train capture made by Sir Francis Drake in 1573.

In just a few years, a maze of mine shafts riddled Potosí. The natives were forced to work in the mines and refining factory. Eventually thousands of natives died from mining accidents, from being worked so hard, and from the mercury used in processing the ore.

Pack trains of llamas carried the raw silver ore to the town at the foot of the mountain where the ore was processed. The silver was then loaded onto mule trains. The mules took the long, long journey over the mountain passes, then through the jungle trails to Cartagena (Colombia) and Portobelo (Panama). In those ports, the silver was loaded onto the Spanish galleons heading for Spain.

The Spanish authorities tried to time the arrival of the silver mule trains to the expected arrival of the Spanish galleons from Spain. These ships were sent out, usually once a year, to collect the riches of the New World and bring them back to Spain. Weather, politics, and other factors often caused them to be late. The treasure was stored in warehouses until the fleet arrived. Pirates often tried to sack these cities when the warehouses were filled with treasure. If the pirates had the wrong information and they hit the town at the wrong time, they just found empty warehouses.

Just a year after the discovery of Potosí, a small group of soldiers and priests made friends with some of the natives in the desert northwest of Mexico City. The Spanish gave gifts of trinkets to the natives. In return, the delighted Spanish were given lumps of silver ore. They found the origin of the silver, and the famous mines of Zacatecas began. More rich deposits were found in Guanajuato and other locations in New Spain (Mexico). The silver from these mines was collected in Mexico City. Then it was carried to the port of Veracruz on the east coast of New Spain to be loaded on the treasure galleons.

At first, gold and silver were sent in the form of bricks and bars. The large bricks were called bullion. The slender bars of silver or gold were called ingots. The Spanish ships carrying the prized metals were the targets of other nations and, above all, pirates.

Mint:

A place where gold and silver are turned into coins.

Soon the Spanish government set up mints to convert the precious metals to coins before shipping to Spain.

The gold and silver in the galleons came in several forms: coins, bars, ingots, works of art, religious objects, and jewelry. The pirates preferred the coins because they were in small in size, and they knew the exact value of the coins. They were the easiest to divvy up with the crew.

Before the discovery of the New World, silver was worth about ⅙ to 1/12 the value of gold. But with a flood of silver

Bullion and Silver Bars:

Ores of gold and silver in bulk amounts is called bullion. These were usually found in the form of bricks and bars of various weights. An average silver bar weighed 70 pounds.

Small thin bars of gold were also called finger bars because of their size.

A lot of gold and silver was smuggled aboard ships to avoid the heavy taxes and tariffs that Spain demanded. Small finger bars were perfect to slip down into a boot cuff, so they were popular for this purpose.

Silver and gold bars are very important to archeologists studying shipwrecks. Besides their actual value in dollars, these treasures can help indicate a wreck's date of loss.

Real Pirate History to Visit:
Treasure to See and Touch
http://www.melfisher.org

In 1622, the Spanish galleons *Nuestra Señora de Atocha* and *Santa Margarita* sank in a hurricane off the Dry Tortugas (off the tip of the Florida Keys). After many determined years of searching, Mel Fisher and his crew found the wreck of the *Santa Margarita* in 1980, and then the *Atocha* in 1985. His search for these wrecks is quite an adventure in itself.

Mel Fisher set up a museum in Key West, Florida, so he could display the treasures and artifacts they recovered from under the sea. There you can see lots and lots of gold and silver (coins, bars, bricks, jewelry, and other items).

Cap'n Michael says:

That Mel Fisher Museum is heaven for a pirate. Lots of treasure. There is even a bar of GOLD that you can pick up. They just don't let you take it—DRAT! Believe me, I tried.

coming into Europe, the value of silver steadily decreased, until in modern times, the value of silver is about $\frac{1}{70}$ the value of gold. The silver the Spanish were bringing to Europe was worth less and less.

Toward the end of the 1700s, the Spanish Empire weakened and began falling apart. It was too weak to hold onto its colonies. One by one the colonies freed themselves from the Empire. In 1825, Simon Bolivar, the great liberator of much of South America, led Peru to its independence. He proclaimed Peru's freedom from the mountaintop of Potosí. The loss of the silver mines of Potosí was a major blow to Spain.

What became of Potosí? The mountain is still there, now in the country of Bolivia (it split off from Peru). The silver is mostly gone now. When the price of silver is high enough, people still dig and bring out a little silver. But the mountain's glory days are in the past. According to official records, more than 45,000 TONS of pure silver was mined from Potosí between 1556 and 1783. That was a LOT of silver.

COINS FOR A PIRATE

You've heard wondrous tales of "Pyrate Treasure"—cargo holds piled high with all manner of gold, silver, and precious jewels just waiting to be taken! But did you ever wonder what that treasure was really like? What sort of treasures would the pirates have found in the New World? Well, we'll tell you about it . . .

When Spanish explorers started finding gold and silver in the Americas, sometimes in huge deposits, it started an out-and-out "gold rush." However, it was actually more like a "silver rush." Gold was much more rare. There was twenty times as much silver as gold in the New World.

Spain quickly set up numerous colonies and started mining the silver and gold. The Spanish conquistadors also started looting all the native empires. They loaded all of this treasure onto Spanish galleons and shipped it back to Spain.

Originally, the silver and gold was melted down and cast into bars and crude bricks before shipping. Then in 1536, the Spanish set up the first silver mint of the Americas in Mexico City. Other mints soon followed it, but only for silver coins. Gold coins were not minted in the New World until 1622.

All this wealth went back to Spain on large Spanish galleons, often lightly protected—just ripe for the picking by an ambitious pirate crew.

All European countries with colonies in the New World (France, Holland, England, etc.) used Spanish coinage as their main currency since Spanish coins were accepted all over the world. A good example is the vessel *Slot ter Hooge* of the Dutch East India Company. She left the Netherlands for Batavia (Indonesia) in the Dutch East Indies. Her cargo contained three tons of silver ingots and four chests of both Dutch coins and Spanish silver coins. She sank in 1724 in the Madeira Islands.

THE PIECE OF EIGHT REALLY WAS MADE OF EIGHT PIECES

The fabled "piece of eight" commonly heard in pirate lore was a silver coin. Its proper Spanish name was *peso de a ocho* (meaning "weight of eight"). It was a coin worth eight *reales* (pronounced "ray-yal-lace"). This was the main silver coin of the Spanish empire. It was originally modeled on the German *taler*, from which is derived the English word "dollar."

A piece of eight was about the same size as an American silver dollar or the Eisenhower dollar coin, but you may not have seen one of those (the new dollar coins are a lot smaller). It was a little bigger than a U.S. Kennedy half-dollar. A piece of eight was worth roughly a dollar back then. But if you happen to have one, don't go selling it for a dollar. They are worth a LOT more now because of their age and history, probably between $100 and $500 depending on their quality and where they are found.

One major drawback of these coins was that a little silver could easily be shaved off

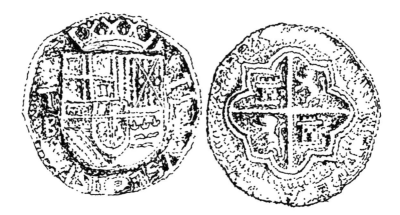

Typical peso worth eight reales, called a piece of eight by the buccaneers. The Hapsburg shield, left, is on the front of the coin and the Crusader's Cross, right, is on the back.

the edges with a blade and no one would know unless they weighed the coin. A little silver shaved off of several coins would give enough silver to make a new coin. The cob-style pieces of eight were melted down and recast into nicely milled coins once they got to Spain (if they made it to Spain).

The piece of eight was so common, it became the basic unit of trade for all the countries and colonies in the New World.

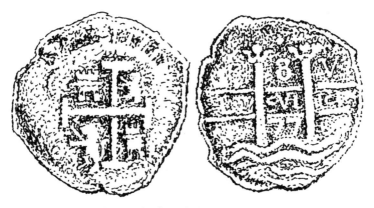

A piece of eight with the Crusader's Cross design on the front and the "pillars and waves" design on the back of the coin.

COINS OF THE SPANISH EMPIRE

Type of Coin	Metal	Value	Notes
Real or **Real de Plata**	Silver		Basic unit for Spanish silver coins. Means "royal." Pronounced "ray-al," not "reel" (plural = reales). Generally came in amounts of 1, 2, 4, and 8 reales.
Peso (peso de a ocho) or "piece of eight"	Silver	= 8 reales	The name means "a weight of 8," but the English mangled this into "pieces of eight." Varied from 22 to 27.5 grams of silver. It was often cut into eight pieces when change was needed.
Escudo	Gold	= 2 pieces of eight = 16 reales	Basic unit for Spanish gold coins. *Escudo* means "shield." At first only minted in Spain. After 1622, it was also minted in Bogotá, New Granada (Colombia).
Double escudo or "doubloon" or "pistole"	Gold	= 2 escudos = 4 pieces of eight = 32 reales	This was called a "doubloon" by the English buccaneers because it was a "double" escudo. However, doubloon became a generic English term for all Spanish gold coins. The French called it a "pistole."
4 Escudo	Gold	= 8 pieces of eight =64 reales	The buccaneers also called this a "double doubloon." Not very common.
8 Escudo	Gold	= 16 pieces of eight = 128 reales	Largest Spanish gold coin. This coin was the same weight as the silver peso (piece of eight). Rare.
Louis d'or or "pistole"	Gold	= 2 escudos	French version of the double escudo.

MAKIN' YER OWN TREASURE CHEST

Start with a large cardboard box, roughly 2 feet wide by 1 foot deep, and about 2 feet high or more.

Cut the sides of the box as shown in Figures 1 and 2 (page 127).

Carefully bend the back over to be the lid for the chest. Don't let it get big creases; try to make lots of little creases as you bend.

At this point, if you plan to paint the cardboard, do so.

Add rope handles as shown in Figure 3.

Cut a strip of cardboard, 6 inches by 1 inch. Bend strip into a U shape as shown in Figure 4. Paint it a metallic color or black.

Cut two slots in the front of the chest, 1 inch high, and wide enough to slide your U-shaped piece of cardboard in. Tape it in place.

Cut two strips of cardboard, 2 inches wide and long enough to go up over the lid, down the back of the chest, under the bottom, and up the front. Paint these a metallic color or black. When dry, glue these in place as shown in Figure 4.

Cut a T-shaped crosspiece, 2 inches high and as wide as the chest is, with a 2-inch-long tab in the center as shown in Figure 4. Paint it the same metallic color or black. When dry, glue in place.

Glue on silver cake-decorating candies for metal studs as shown in Figure 5 (page 128).

TWO BITS, FOUR BITS, SIX BITS, A DOLLAR

The peso was often cut into eight pieces in order to make smaller change. Special coin shears (scissors) or a chisel and hammer were used to cut the coin. Each piece was called a "bit." Half a coin was four bits, a quarter of a coin was two bits. "Two bits" is also a slang word for the U.S. 25-cent piece, as in the famous saying "Shave and a haircut, two bits."

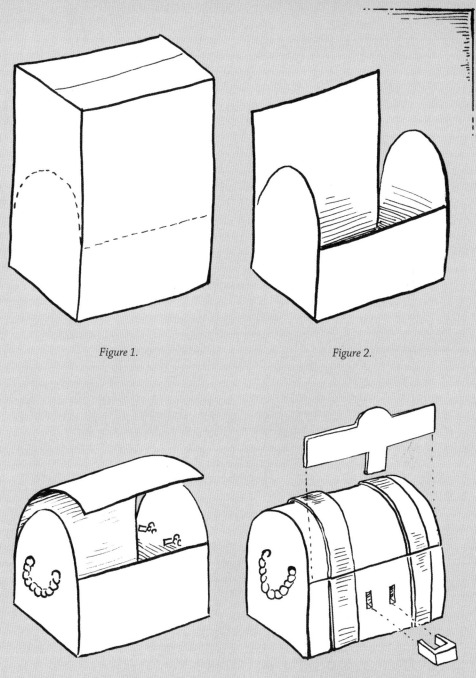

Figure 1.

Figure 2.

Figure 3.

Figure 4.

MAKIN' YER OWN TREASURE CHEST

(Continued)

Figure 5.

MAKIN' YER OWN PIECES OF EIGHT

Now that you've made your own Treasure Chest, you are going to need lots of pieces of eight to fill it. Cut circles of cardboard about 1½ to 2 inches in diameter. Cover them with aluminum foil or paint them silver.

FISHING FOR SILVER AND GOLD

Back in the 1600s and early 1700s, the Spanish were happily ravaging the New World for its wealth and sending it back to Spain. The silver, gold, and other riches were sent back to Spain in fleets of ships that usually sailed once a year. The treasure ships traveled together for safety and protection from pirate attacks. But traveling in groups did not protect fragile wooden ships from the terrible might of a hurricane.

By the summer of 1715, Spain had been at war with various European countries for a few years. Due to the number of enemy ships sailing off the Spanish coast, it had been too dangerous to send the treasure fleet across the Atlantic. However, fighting a war was expensive. The Spanish crown's treasury was in frantic need of new funds. Once the peace treaty was signed, there was pressure for the treasure fleet to sail right away, even though hurricane season (June to November) had already begun.

On July 24, 1715, the treasure fleet (*flota*) consisting of ten Spanish ships and one French ship left Havana, Cuba. Together the Spanish ships had about 14 MILLION pesos worth of silver and gold coins. There were also gold bars, gold dust, emeralds, pearls, jewelry, and precious Chinese porcelain that had been brought all the way from the Philippines.

As was usual, the fleet headed north, hugging the east coast of Florida. For the first five days, everything went smoothly. Then, on July 29, the waves changed into long swells. Experienced sailors became worried. They knew the signs of a coming storm.

On July 30, the winds were getting stronger. By afternoon, the waves were more than twenty feet high. The strong winds pushed the ships west, closer and closer to the Florida coast. The captain general ordered that the ships head straight into the wind to keep clear of the reefs near the coast, but the winds were too strong.

At about 4 a.m. on July 31, the deadly hurricane struck with its full force, driving one ship after another into the reefs. The treasure ships were shattered and their crews had little chance. All the ships were lost and, of the 2,500 people aboard, about one thousand were killed.

As daylight broke later that morning, the survivors looked around. The Florida beaches between present-day Cape Canaveral and Fort Pierce were littered with wreckage and bodies. The various ships had come ashore at different locations, often miles apart.

For those who survived the shipwrecks, their ordeal was not over. They were stranded in a land filled with mosquitoes, rattlesnakes, alligators, wild animals, and hostile Native Americans. Most of their food, water, and medical supplies had been lost in the storm.

Admiral Don Francisco Salmon sent a small boat with nineteen men back to Cuba for help. Ten days later they reached Havana.

After a couple of days to prepare, several rescue ships set out. They were filled with emergency supplies, salvage equipment, and men. After they arrived at the wreck site, even more help arrived from the Spanish settlement at St. Augustine in northern Florida.

Salvage began right away because Spain still needed that treasure. The wrecks were mostly in shallow water. By dragging the ocean bottom with

Pirates in the Movies: Henry Jennings' Raid

The documentary *True Caribbean Pirates* depicts a thrilling version of Henry Jennings' raid on the Spanish salvage camp.

nets, they were able to bring up chests of coins. Divers were sent down to recover the treasure that had escaped the nets. By early 1716, the salvagers had fished up about 80 percent of the lost treasure.

News of the wrecks and the sunken riches spread through the Americas and Europe like wildfire, and sparking the imagination and greed of others. Pirates, privateers, and treasure hunters the world over swooped down on the Florida coast like vultures, hoping to recover some of the treasure before the Spanish could get it all.

The pirate Henry Jennings was one of the first "vultures" to arrive. He came with three ships and three hundred men in January 1716. Rather than diving for treasure, he decided on an easier way. He and his men swooped down on a salvage camp on the beach and looted some 120,000 pieces of eight that had been brought ashore. They also stole four of the Spanish cannons.

More would-be looters arrived. The nearby islands of the Bahamas filled with these rogues, many of whom stayed in the area, even when they were unsuccessful in getting a share of the lost treasure. The small pirate settlement on New Providence swelled with the new arrivals. The names of some of them read like a Pirates' Who's Who, including Blackbeard, Benjamin Hornigold, Charles Vane, and Jack Rackham.

Real Pirate History to Visit:

The 1715 Spanish Fleet Shipwreck Camp

You can visit the site of the beach camp made by the 1715 Spanish Plate Fleet survivors. This is also the site of the salvaging efforts. The McLarty Treasure Museum is there now. They have lots of Spanish treasure on display: gold and silver coins, Chinese porcelain, jewelry, and more. There are also swords and flintlocks, along with tools left behind by the salvage crews. The museum is part of the Sebastian Inlet State Park.

McLarty Treasure Museum
13180 North Highway A1A
Vero Beach, FL 32963
772-589-2147
www.atocha1622.com/mclarty.htm

LEAVE THE TREASURE TO US

To get ready for salvaging lost treasure the next time a gold- and silver-filled galleon sinks in a hurricane, here is a game you can practice in the swimming pool.
You'll need:

† ten pennies and two dimes (or replica Spanish treasure coins)
  † a swimming pool
    † a grownup lifeguard

Pennies and dimes are fine, but pieces of eight and doubloons are better. You can find replicas of these coins at many of the pirate stores and online pirate supply companies. We have a list of these at www.noquartergiven.net/merchant.htm

Make sure you have a grownup lifeguard on hand. Throw all the coins into your pool. Throw them into the shallow end to start. See how many you can get in one dive (that means in ONE breath, just like the divers of old who retrieved sunken treasure). Dimes are worth five times as much as the pennies.

After the first person dives, throw the coins back into the same area, and the next person takes a turn. After everyone takes a turn, add up the points to see who retrieved the most treasure. Winner is the diver with the most points.

ADD DIFFICULTY: To make a harder challenge, thrown the coins into deeper and deeper water.

ONE PERSON PLAY: If you don't have your crew along, you can still play. After each turn, add up your points. See if you can get better. If you can pick up all twelve coins, try doubling the amount of coins you throw. (Even if you are playing the game by yourself, make sure there is a grownup lifeguard watching you.)

NOTE: When you are done, make sure you get all of your coins out of the pool. No self-respectin' pirate would leave treasure behind. Besides, some innocent little sea turtle might come along and swallow them, and that would not be good for its digestion.

HOIST YER COLORS

PASS WITH FLYING COLORS!

ost people think pirates all flew the same "Jolly Roger," a black flag with a skull and crossbones on it, but that's not true. In the 1600s, most privateers (and some pirates) flew either their national flag or the flag of the nation that gave them their letter of marque. Privateers also flew a special pennant or streamer that identified them as a privateer. Pirates originally flew a blood red flag called the "Red Jack" or the "Bloody Flag." The red flag meant "No Quarter Given," or no mercy unless you surrendered immediately without a fight. Even then, there was no guarantee that you would receive good treatment.

Cap'n Michael says:

When it comes to pirate flags, most people don't know jack!
Let the ol' Cap'n tell you how it really was.

It IS a mite confusing, all those flags flyin' on a vessel.
Let's see if I can clear things up a bit. First off, sailors didn't usually call 'em flags. Instead, they called them their colours (that's how the British spell "colors"). They had special names for different kinds of colours, depending where they were flown on the ship.

On the stern (the back) of the vessel, they had a flagpole called an ensign staff. Flags flown from this pole were (you guessed it!) called ensigns. This is one of the two main places where pirates flew their special Jolly Roger flags. They also flew Jolly Rogers from the end of the gaff (the pole holding the top of the large sail on the last mast). From this staff, navy warships would fly a naval ensign showing the country and squadron they were in. (British navy warships had red, white, and blue ensigns for the Red, White, or Blue squadrons).

There was a very long flag called a pennant (also called a pendant or pendent) flown from the top of the tallest mast on the ship. Pennants might be found at the tops of other masts as well. Pirates were known to fly black pennants either with or without symbols on them. Pennants might come to a point or might be forked, with two long points on them. Pirates also flew a red pennant to show "No Quarter" (no mercy) would be given. Privateers flew a special red privateers pennant, and warships flew a variety of pennants.

On the front of vessels, usually fastened to the bowsprit, was a flagpole called the jack staff. The national flag of their country was usually flown from this staff. Some pirates flew their national flag here. The flags flown from this flagpole were (you guessed it again) called jacks. (This is why the British national flag is often called the Union Jack).

Of course, this was the general custom regarding flags. Pirates might have followed these customs, or they might have done whatever they wanted. They were pirates, after all.

Vessel:

A general term for any large craft that travels on water.

Bowsprit:

A pole sticking out from the bow (front) of a vessel. It supports the small triangular sails out in front.

A favorite trick of the pirates was to sail under some other flag, usually the flag of their victim. Pirates were familiar with the look of vessels from different countries. If they recognized it as a Spanish merchant ship, they would go to the flag locker, select a Spanish flag, and run it up the mast (well-equipped pirates would carry flags of all the countries sailing in

Craft

(nautical):
Any ship or boat on the water.

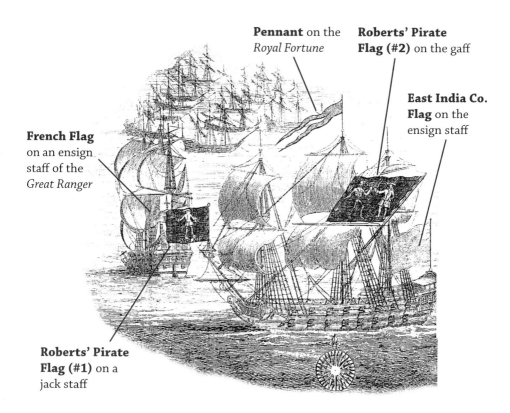

Pennant on the *Royal Fortune*

Roberts' Pirate Flag (#2) on the gaff

East India Co. Flag on the ensign staff

French Flag on an ensign staff of the *Great Ranger*

Roberts' Pirate Flag (#1) on a jack staff

Bartholomew Roberts' flagship, the Royal Fortune, *and the* Great Ranger *are shown flying several flags, including two of Roberts' pirate flags, an English East India Company flag, and a French national flag. In the background are eleven slave ships Roberts held for ransom.*

the area). This was known as "flying false colors." Lulled into a false sense of security, the Spanish merchant would allow them to approach. The custom of ships from the same country or other friendly nations meeting at sea was to exchange greetings, mail, or news of home with each other. When the pirate was close enough to attack, down would come the false colors and up would go the Red Jack.

More rarely, pirates flew a plain black flag instead of the red. When Francis Drake raided Cartagena (on the coast of modern-day Colombia) in 1585, it was recorded that he was "flying black banners and streamers, menacing war to the death."

The first recorded sighting of a pirate flying the Jolly Roger was of the French fili-buster Emanuel Wynne's colors in 1700. After that time, the black flag was adopted by most pirates sailing in the Caribbean area (West Indies). They used various menacing symbols on it. This black flag had a different message than the red flag: "When they [the pirates] fight under Jolly Roger, they give quarter which they do not when they fight under the Red Flag" (Captain Richard Hawkins, 1724). Instead of a death threat, the pirates now offered mercy to all—as long as they cooperated. A victim was supposed to "strike their colors" (lower their flag) and surrender immediately.

What happened if you didn't surrender immediately is shown by Article 10 in the charter-party (ship's articles) of French filibuster Captain Dulaïen:

Article 10: If the vessels which we attack defend themselves under the black flag, and then after hoisting the red flag, they fire three times upon us, no quarter shall be given to any aboard them.

In other words, if they resist after the red flag is raised, kill them all. A bloody flag indeed.

Many pirate captains personalized their flags with their own individual designs. There were two reasons for this. First, they wanted their victim to know they were being attacked by a pirate, not a privateer or government vessel. You could fight back against a privateer and still expect humane treatment, because privateers had to obey laws regarding how they treated prisoners. Fighting back against pirates was much riskier. They would normally show no mercy to those who continued to resist them.

Second, the flag identified which particular captain you were facing. It made sense that pirates would want to personalize their flags. After all, no self-respecting pirate would want to fly a flag just like everybody else's. His flag was his signature. He would want it to be special and distinctive so everyone would know it was HIS flag. He also wanted it to be as scary as possible to strike terror into the hearts of his victims. The flags usually featured skulls, bones, bleeding hearts, or other grisly objects with special symbolic meanings. Their message was clear: "Surrender or Die!"

One of the few flag designs that is well documented is that of Captain John Thomas Dulaïen. He surrendered to French authorities in 1729 and accepted the king's pardon. The illustration on page 136 is from the French archives. It shows the Jolly Roger that Captain Dulaïen flew from his ship as well as his bloody red "no quarter" flags.

There are a lot of opinions about which flags the various pirate captains flew. Very

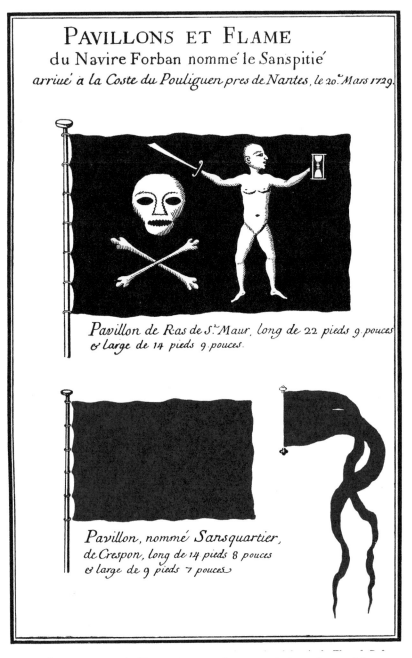

PAVILLONS ET FLAME
du Navire Forban nommé le Sanspitié
arrivé à la Coste du Pouliguen pres de Nantes, le 20.ᵉ Mars 1729.

Pavillon de Ras de S.ᵗ Maur, long de 22 pieds 9 pouces & large de 14 pieds 9 pouces.

Pavillon, nommé Sansquartier, de Crespon, long de 14 pieds 8 pouces & large de 9 pieds 7 pouces

Jolly Roger of French filibuster Captain John Thomas Dulaïen along with his bloody red "no quarter" flags, flown aboard his vessel Le Sanspitie (Without Pity).

few of the original pirate flags still exist. Many pirates were proud of their flags and viewed them as a symbol of their freedom. They usually destroyed their flags rather than risk them being captured.

An account of the capture of one of Bartholomew Roberts' vessels describes the attitude of the pirate crew toward their colors. "The colours were thrown over-board, that they might not rise in Judgment, nor be display'd in Triumph over them."

Of the few flags that were captured, most were not preserved. Eyewitness accounts were often vague: "The pyrate flag was a deaths head." (A death's head could be a skull, a skull with crossbones below it, a skull with other symbols next to it, etc.) Sometimes eyewitness accounts conflicted, or they might have been mistaken about whom the flag belonged to.

British Admiralty records give us the first actual account of a pirate captain's flag. Captain John Cranby of the HMS *Poole* engaged the infamous French pirate Emanuel Wynne off the Cape Verde islands in the year 1700. Captain Cranby chased Wynne's vessel into a cove at Brava Island, where he thought he had Wynne trapped, but a group of Portuguese soldiers came to Wynne's aid and he managed to escape. Captain Cranby described Wynne's flag as "a sable (black) ensign with cross bones, a death's head and an hourglass."

Cap'n Michael says:

There's been all kind's o' tales about where they got the name "Jolly Roger" fer a pirate flag. Maybe the old Captain can shed a bit o' light on the subject.

A lot of the early buccaneers were Frenchmen, and they liked to call their bloody red flag the *joli rouge* (pretty red), which some believe is the origin of the name "Jolly Roger." Another tale gives a famous southern Indian pirate the credit. His name was Ali Raja and he flew a red flag as well. The English sailors started calling him and his flag the Ally Roger, which over time could easily have turned into the Jolly Roger. Now me own favorite theory has ta do with a bit of English slang. Our nickname for the devil was "Old Roger," and we'd often draw him as a skeleton or some such. Old Roger was used as part of the design of many a pirate flag. And so a Jolly Roger would have been a happy devil. Which sounds ta me like an appropriate description for the sort of mischief that us pirates got into.

Anyway, whatever the truth of it, the name stuck, and pirate flags are still called Jolly Rogers to this day.

BLEEDING HEARTS AND WINGED HOURGLASSES:
PIRATE FLAG SYMBOLS AND THEIR MEANINGS

Pirates liked to decorate their flags with many different symbols. But I bet ya didn't know that those symbols all had special meanings. Below we explain the various symbols, and what pirates were "saying" with them.

Arm holding a knife or sword: We are powerful fighters, ready to fight and kill.

Axe: Destruction.

Black spot: Our victims are marked for death, doomed. (The idea of a "black spot" seems to have come from the book *Treasure Island*. There is no record of historical pirates using this symbol.)

Blazing cannonballs: The terror of battle, destruction.

Crossbones: You (our victims) can die any time. Soon you will be nothing but bones.

Goblet raised: A toast to Death.

Grim Reaper: A skeleton or hooded figure holding a curved blade on a handle (scythe). The Spirit of Death. Death has come for you.

Heart: Heartache and sorrow.

Heart dripping blood: You will have a slow, agonizing death; torture.

Hourglass: Time is running out for you; your life will be short.

Initials: might be your own initials or those of your enemy. (As in Bartholomew Roberts' flag below. Roberts hated Barbados and Martinique because the governors of those two islands had tried to capture him. The flag shows Roberts standing on two skulls. The initials ABH and AMH stand for "A Barbadian's Head" and "A Martinician's Head.")

Bartholomew Roberts' flag.

Knife/dagger: We are ready to fight.

Man: If clothed, usually represents the captain of the pirates.

Man holding up knife: We are ready to fight and kill; powerful fighters.

Naked man: Without shame.

Scythe (curved blade on a handle): The Grim Reaper's tool to harvest souls.

Skeleton: King Death and the shortness of life. Also can be the devil.

Skeleton dancing: We delight in death and don't care what happens to us.

Skeleton, horned: Represents the devil, also called "Old Roger." (There is one of these on Blackbeard's flag.) Your time has run out. The devil himself has come for you, and you will suffer a slow, painful death.

Skeleton, red: Bloody, violent death. A lot of blood will be spilled, and a lot of people will die.

Skull: Symbolizes death. On gravestones, skulls were usually drawn with wings, showing the soul was going to heaven. By leaving the wings off, pirates were saying your soul would go

to meet with the devil instead. Pirates would swear an oath over a skull, believing if they broke their oath, they would die.

Skull over crossbones: Called the "death's head," this was a common symbol for death. Sea captains often used this symbol to record a death in their logbooks. Pirates used it to say, "We are death! Defy us and die."

Skull held up by hand: We celebrate and welcome death.

Spear: We are ready for battle. You will die if you fight us.

Swords crossed: Death during battle.

Swords: Power, violence, and aggression. Pirates often swore an oath upon a sword.

Sword in flames: Defiance.

Winged hourglass: Your time to live is flying away.

A BLACK FLAG WOULD BE AS GOOD AS FIFTY MEN

Now that you understand what the symbols on the flags mean, it's time to get creative and design a flag of your own.

THE FIELD

Lets start by picking out the background color on the flag. This was commonly called the field.

Black Field: During the early 1700s, black was the preferred color, but there were a few red flags. Henry Every (also known as John Avery) flew both black and red versions of his flag, and Christopher Moody had a red flag as well. Black represents death, darkness, and terror.

Red Field: Red means "No Quarter Given," or no mercy (quarter) shown to anyone. Red represents blood, violence, battle, and danger.

White Field: Though a white flag could mean "surrender," it was also the flag of France in the 1600s. There is an account of a white flag with a black "death's head." The pirate might have been French.

Other colors were rarely used.

LAYOUT

Once you have picked your background color, your next step is to select your symbols. Go back and look over the symbols in the previous section. You may use these or other symbols that have special meaning for you. Pick the ones that you think will look best together on your flag. We recommend between two and six symbols. More than that and your flag will look too crowded. And remember, your symbols don't all have to be white; some could be red, gold, or any other color you choose.

Draw your design on a piece of paper. With a little thought and some creative arranging, you can design a flag that is uniquely your own. Later in this chapter, we'll show you how to make your design into a flag.

FAMOUS PIRATES AND THEIR FLAGS

N ow that you've designed your own Jolly Roger, lets take a look at some more infamous pirate captains and see how they designed theirs.

CHRISTOPHER CONDENT

Christopher Condent was one of the more successful pirates of the eighteenth century. In 1720, near Bombay, India, Condent's ship, the *Flying Dragon*, captured a huge Arabic vessel containing more than £150,000 ($375 million dollars) in treasure and valuables. Deciding it was a good time to retire, he set sail for the French island of Reunion, where he took the king's pardon, married the governor's sister-in-law, and settled down to become a wealthy merchant.

Condent's flag was said to be the traditional skull and crossbones repeated three times across the banner. This flag was also used as a generic pirate pennant, usually flown from the topmast of the vessel, with the pirate's personal flag flown from the rearmost (or mizzen) mast.

There seems to be no eyewitness accounts of what flag Condent flew. One early 1900s historian says this design dates to 1704, but he did not assign it to any certain pirate.

EDWARD LOWE

Captain Edward Lowe (alias Ned Low) was one of the most brutal and sadistic pirates of the early 1700s. He inflicted torture and did many cruel things to his victims. The only people he treated decently were married men. Since he missed his own daughter terribly, he refused to "force" married men into his crew, saying he would make no child an orphan.

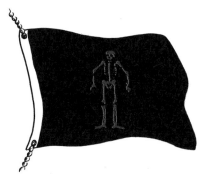

An eyewitness described Lowe's flag as "a Black Flag with a figure of death [a skeleton] in red." This was a fittingly bloodthirsty banner for one of history's most bloodthirsty pirates. Lowe had more than one flag. It was also reported he flew a flag similar to the one described for Blackbeard.

Lowe even had a flag for special occasions. He was said to have used a green silk flag with a yellow figure of a man blowing a trumpet. The Green Trumpeter flag was used when several pirate ships sailed together as a fleet. The flag was hoisted to the top of the mizzenmast to call his captains to a meeting aboard the flagship.

CHRISTOPHER MOODY

Christopher Moody was one of Bartholomew Roberts' officers. But a few years before sailing with Roberts, he had been a captain in his own right. He mainly pirated off the coast of North and South Carolina.

His flag was red like the older "bloody" flags. It featured a gold, winged hourglass, showing victims that their time to live was flying away. In addition, there was an arm holding a dagger and a gold skull with crossbones. He also liked to fly a red pennant from the top of the mainmast.

This design may not be Moody's. There seems to be no eyewitness record of what flag Moody actually flew. A flag design similar to this was first described in the late 1700s as just being a pirate flag. So we know pirates used the design. We are just not sure which pirate used it.

JOHN QUELCH

John Quelch sailed from Marblehead, Massachusetts, as part of a privateering crew. They quickly mutinied and elected John as their captain. Quelch sailed for the coast of Brazil, where he captured nine Portuguese vessels and a great quantity of treasure. They foolishly sailed back to Marblehead to sell their ill-gotten gains, where they were quickly captured.

Quelch's flag was described as "an anatomy [naked man] with an hourglass in one hand and a dart in the heart with three drops of blood proceeding from it in the other." It is often confused with Blackbeard's flag, which is very similar.

The first description of this flag for Quelch seems to be from a historian in 1911. There is no mention of it in any of the trial records. At Quelch's trial, it was reported he would fly the English colors throughout his attacks. This was the trick he used to make his victims think his was a friendly ship . . . until too late.

THOMAS TEW

Thomas Tew was commissioned by the governor of Bermuda to raid French trading posts along the African coast. But Tew had different plans—to turn pirate! When he informed his crew of his decision, they were said to have shouted, "A gold chain or a wooden leg, we'll stand by you!" He set sail for the Red Sea in search of treasure. And he succeeded beyond his wildest dreams! He managed to capture one of the Grand Moghul's ships filled with gold, ivory, silks, and other treasure worth over $50 million dollars by some accounts.

Tew was not satisfied with this fortune. He went back to the Red Sea for more, but he would pay for his greed. Tew was killed when his vessel, along with John Avery's *Fancy* and two others, attacked the Grand Moghul's treasure fleet. A shot got him in the belly.

Tew's flag is a white arm holding a sword, on a black field, meaning "We are ready to kill you!" It is doubtful Thomas Tew actually used this flag. He died in 1695, five years before the first black and white pirate flags were reported being used. However, the symbol of the arm holding the sword was a common design used in the 1600s.

RICHARD WORLEY

Richard Worley set out from New York in 1718 with a crew of eight men to become a pirate. They terrorized the American colonies and the Bahamas for a short time. His career lasted less than a year before he was killed in battle near Jamestown, Virginia, in February 1719. His crew was captured and hanged.

This design might be accurate, for an eyewitness said Worley had a black flag "with a white Death's Head in the Middle of it." Though this does not mention the crossed bones behind the head, they may have been there, or an inventive artist could have added them later.

EMANUEL WYNNE

Emanuel Wynne, a French pirate of the 1700s, was the first pirate known to have flown his own personalized black flag.

On July 18, 1700, the HMS *Poole*, commanded by Captain John Cranby, engaged Wynne's ship off the Cape Verde Islands. In Cranby's account, he described "a sable ensign with cross bones, a death's head, and an hour glass." The hourglass was a common pirate symbol signifying that only by surrendering quickly could his prey evade death.

FLYING YER COLORS

N ow that you've designed your own flag, here are some ways to make your pirate flag fly. Discuss with your parents which method you wish to use (appliqué, paint, or bleach gel pen).

TYPE OF CLOTH

Pirate flags were often said to be silk. Silk is lightweight and catches the wind nicely, but silk can be rather expensive. A plain cotton fabric is fine too. To save money, try finding some plain cotton sheets at a thrift or discount store (avoid those that are a cotton/polyester mix if you plan to use the bleach gel pen method). If you can't find the color you need, get white or light solid-colored 100 percent cotton sheets and dye them the color you want. Be sure to get help from your parents with the dye. (Dyes work best on 100 percent cotton. Avoid cotton/polyester blends.)

CUTTING THE CLOTH AND HEMMING

Decide if your flag should be one layer or two layers back-to-back sewn together. A single-layer flag will be lighter and will catch the wind easier than a double-layer flag. It also uses less fabric, so it is cheaper to make.

For the bleach method, you can make your flag from only one layer of cloth. The design will show through on both sides, but one side will be in reverse (mirror image) from the other. The appliqué and painting methods can also work with one layer, but you will need to paint or apply your design to both sides (if the paint shows through the fabric, you will need to use two layers). Again, the sides will be reverse images from each other. Perhaps you plan to display your flag so only one side will show. Then you will only need one layer because it won't matter how the reverse side looks.

If you want the design on both sides to appear the same, you will need to make two flags, and sew them back-to-back. If you have letters or words in your design, this will be necessary.

One Layer: When you cut your fabric into a rectangle, you will need 3 inches extra on the left side of the design to make a pocket for the pole. Add 1 inch extra on the remaining three edges of your fabric. You can do the hemming (fold over and hide the raw edges) before or after you make the design.

FLYING YER COLORS

(Continued)

First, fold the fabric over along each edge ½ inch and sew it down. Then fold each edge another ½ inch and sew again. This way, all raw edges are on the inside, to prevent unraveling. (If you don't know how to use a sewing machine or don't have one, get help from someone who does. Or, you can hand-sew the hems.)

Two Layers: You will need to cut two separate rectangles for your flag. When you measure it, you will need 3 inches extra on the left side of the fabric to make a pocket for the pole. Add an extra ⅝ inch along each of the other three edges for the seam (where the pieces are sewed together). You will need to wait until you are done making the design before you sew the two sides together. When you sew them together, put them face to face and sew around all the sides at ⅝ inch from the edges. Leave about an 8-inch gap on one side to turn the flag right-side out. Before you turn it, clip off each corner close to the stitching without cutting the stitches. This will let the corners lay flat after you turn them inside out. Turn it right side out and iron the edges flat with a warm iron. Hand-sew the open gap closed.

APPLIQUÉ

You will need:

- † Cloth for your flag background
- † Cloth for your flag design (white or other colors your design calls for)
- † Chalk
- † Scissors
- † Needle and thread, or sewing machine, or fabric glue

In this method, you will cut your design out of the white or other color cloth and sew or glue it on the flag.

Sketch out your design on your white or other color fabric using a piece of colored chalk. Remember, if you want the design to show on both sides of your flag, you will need to make two sets of your design.

Cut out your design with the scissors, carefully following your chalk lines.

Glue or sew the design pieces onto the background cloth. If you are using a sewing machine, use the zigzag mode to help keep the raw edges of the cloth from unraveling.

Glue or sew the second set of design pieces onto the backside of the cloth (for a one-layer flag) or on the second background cloth (for a two-layer flag).

FLYING YER COLORS

(Continued)

PAINTING

You will need:

† Cloth for your flag
† Chalk
† Acrylic paint
† Round or chisel-shaped paint brush
    (1 inch or smaller diameter)
† Rag to wipe with
† Rinse water cup
† Old newspapers or paper bags

You can paint onto the cloth with acrylic craft paints. Once they dry they are permanent, so be careful. Even before they dry, they are hard to get out of unwanted places.

Be sure to cover your work surface with old newspapers or used paper bags. You should wear old clothes.

Sketch out your design on your cloth using a piece of chalk. Remember, if you are making a two-layered flag, you will need to draw your design on both pieces.

Paint your design following your chalk drawing. Be careful not to get paint on you or on other things. While the paint is drying, rinse out your brushes with soap and water. Dump out the rinse water and clean the cup.

If you are making a one-layered flag, you will need to wait until the first side is completely dry before flipping the flag over to paint the other side.

If you are making a two-layered flag, paint both pieces of fabric. When they are both completely dry, you can sew them together as described on page 147.

BLEACH PEN

You will need:

- † Cloth for your flag
- † Chalk
- † Gel bleach pen (Clorox Bleach Pen) OR Rit Color Remover
- † Stop-Bleach (or hydrogen peroxide)
- † Tub
- † Plastic or paper bags or old newspapers

With a gel bleach pen, you can draw your design right onto the black or colored fabric. The color on the cloth erases away. This works on 100 percent cotton or linen cloth only! The bleach has been thickened into a gel so it is easier to use and less messy than unthickened bleach. Depending on how big your design is, you might need more than one gel bleach pen.

Depending on the fabric and how it was colored, you will get different results. Instead of white, it might turn to a light color (black often turns light reddish-brown or orange). Not all fabrics and dyes will work well with this method. Use this only for COTTON and LINEN cloth. DO NOT USE THIS ON SILK OR MAN-MADE FABRICS (including cotton/polyester blends). If you want your flag to be silk, you can use Rit Color Remover instead (this will also work for cotton or linen).

WARNING

Check with your parents before you start. You will need their supervision and help with this project.

Be sure to cover your work surface with plastic or used paper bags or old newspapers. You should wear old clothes. Be careful not to get bleach drips on your clothes or the things around you. Bleach spots are PERMANENT.

First, test the fabric to make sure it is able to lose color. Shake the pen and start squeezing gently. Make a small mark on a fabric scrap with the bleach pen. Beware of accidental drips! If the color disappears, good. If it does not disappear, you will need to get different cloth or try the sewing or painting methods.

Have your parents help you prepare a stop-bleach bath. You will need to have this ready to rinse the cloth in the stop-bleach bath right after you finish drawing your design. If you don't use the stop-bleach, the bleach (a mild acid) will eat away at your fabric, and, after a while, holes will show up. You can use Anti-Chlor, Bleach Stop, or some other bleach neutralizer (available where you buy dyes) as your stop-bleach bath. Follow the instructions on the package. Instead, you can soak the cloth with 3 percent hydrogen peroxide (the kind you get in drug stores). Hydrogen peroxide costs more than Anti-Chlor, but it is safe and it works. Use one part hydrogen peroxide to eight parts water.

Sketch out your design on your cloth using a piece of chalk.

Use the bleach pen to draw your design. Watch out for accidental drips. Be aware that, the longer the bleach sits on the cloth, the more it lightens, but it also continues to spread the design wider.

After you finish drawing your design and the color has been removed to the way you want it, rinse the cloth in water right away.

Next, put it in the stop-bleach bath and follow the instructions on the package. If you are using hydrogen peroxide, let the fabric sit in the mixture for five minutes or more.

Rinse with clean water and let the cloth sit in the clean water for ten minutes or more.

Lay your flag out flat to dry.

POCKET FOR THE POLE

After you have hemmed the edges of your flag (for a one-layer flag) or sewn the two layers together, you can make a pocket for a pole. Fold over the fabric 1 inch on the left side to make a pocket. Sew it down along the edge. Sew it closed across the top. Slide the flag onto a ¾-inch diameter wooden dowel.

VARIATION:

You can put metal rings (grommets) in two of the corners of your flag to attach it with ropes to a flagpole. If you (or someone you know) have a grommet tool, then sew down the pocket on top AND bottom (so it is closed). Put a grommet near the top left corner, through the extra layers formed by the folded-over pocket (these extra layers will give it more strength from pulling out easily). Put a second grommet near the bottom left corner.

NOTE: Grommet is also a term for a ship's boy.

GIVE 'EM A BROADSIDE!

> **TAKE YER BEST SHOT!**

"The *Arabella* seemed to explode as she swept by. Eighteen guns from each of her flanks emptied themselves at that point-blank range into the hulls of the two Spanish vessels. . . . From the grim confusion and turmoil in the waist below arose a clamor of fierce Spanish blasphemies and the screams of maimed men. The *Milagrosa* staggered slowly ahead, a gaping rent in her bulwarks; her foremast was shattered, fragments of the yards hanging in the netting spread below. Her beak-head was in splinters and a shot had smashed through into the great cabin, reducing it to wreckage."

—From *Captain Blood*, by Raphael Sabatini

CANNONS THROUGH THE AGES

Even though the Chinese first invented gunpowder, the Moors were the ones who first brought cannons to Western Europe.

RING AND STAVE CANNON

The fourteenth century is when cannons first showed up on European ships. One of the earliest designs was called a ring and stave cannon. There were two main types of these early shipboard cannons.

The first type was made up of wrought-iron bars welded together to form a tube. You could imagine a blacksmith of old, sweat pouring down his brow, as he worked away over his forge.

For the second type of ring and stave cannon, a thick sheet of iron was bent around a rod to form a tube. It was then heated and welded together. This tube was surrounded by a single layer of widely spaced heavy iron rings that were shrunk in place over the tube.

Firing the ring and stave cannon.

In either case, the resulting gunbarrel was bolted down to a heavy rectangular oak
bed that had been grooved to receive it. The rear of the barrel was closed off. Just forward of this point an opening was cut into the top of the barrel. This opening was called
a breech.

This type of cannon was a breech-loader. It was loaded from the rear end. The
gun crew could quickly load it using a removable round chamber that fit into the
cutaway breech.

MUZZLE LOADING CANNON

The first major improvement in cannon design came in 1543 when they started casting
cannon as one piece instead of building them up from smaller pieces. These cannon
were the muzzleloaders (front-loading cannons). The workers cast the cannon as a solid
piece, then drilled out the bore (the hollow inside) using treadmill or water-powered
drills. A touchhole (for lighting the powder) was drilled out by hand after the cannon
was finished.

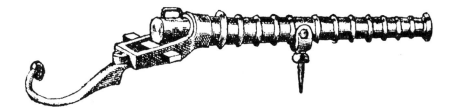

Second type of ring and stave cannon, in the form of a swivel gun.

Parts of the Cannon

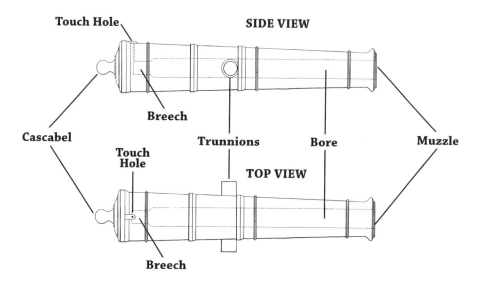

Touch Hole
SIDE VIEW
Breech
Cascabel
Touch Hole
Trunnions
Bore
Muzzle
TOP VIEW
Breech

Cannons were made from cast iron (a mixture of iron, carbon, and silicon), brass, or bronze. Bronze was preferred for shipboard cannons. It was lighter than iron, it didn't rust as much, and when the cannons wore out, the metal could be easily recast to make new ones. The disadvantage was that bronze cannons were twice as expensive.

Cap'n Michael says:

There's some confusion between the words "cannon" and "gun." Dependin' on who's talkin', both words are used to describe them big iron or bronze monstrosities onboard ship. I ain't sayin' which one is correct, but gun is probably more proper for the shipboard weapons.

And if there is more than one of them (which ya really need if yer goin' into battle), then ya can call them cannon or cannons. Both ways are correct. Also, it was sometimes spelt with only one "n" in the middle: "canon." And ya wonder why I have problems spellin'!

Real Pirate History to Visit:
Castillo de San Marcos, St. Augustine, Florida

St. Augustine is the oldest European-founded city in the United States. This is a great spot to get a glimpse of the pirate era. The seventeenth-century fortress was attacked a couple of times by pirates, including Robert Searles. The fort still looks pretty much as it did in those times. The big cannons are still there and are fired on special occasions. Outside the fort, you'll find the Taberna del Gallo nearby at 35 St. George Street. It's a 1740s Spanish tavern with no electricity, just flickering candles. Hang around; the city's nightly ghost tour starts at the Taberna in the evening.

800-653-2489
www.getaway4florida.com
http://ghosttoursofstaugustine.com

Cutaway View of a 32-pound Naval Cannon

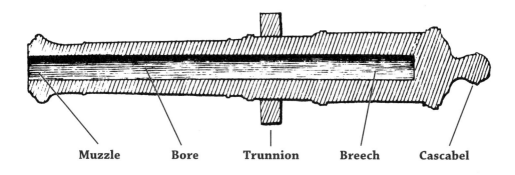

Muzzle   **Bore**   **Trunnion**   **Breech**   **Cascabel**

CARRONADES

The next major improvement in cannon design came with the invention of the carronade, first produced by the Scottish foundries of Carron in 1779. This piece threw a very large shot from a stubby barrel. These carronades needed a much smaller powder charge, and at short range they were more accurate than regular cannon. Carronades came in many sizes. Some larger man-of-war carried carronades capable of firing a 68-pound ball!

Types of Cannon

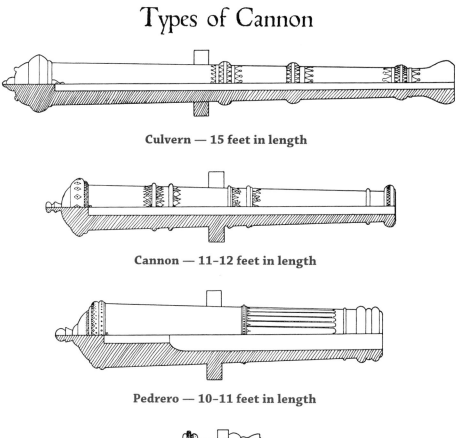

Culvern — 15 feet in length

Cannon — 11–12 feet in length

Pedrero — 10–11 feet in length

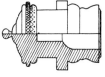

Mortar — 3 feet in length

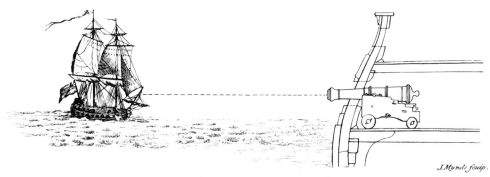

Aiming the cannon at an enemy vessel.

J.Mynde fculp.

SWIVEL GUNS

Swivel guns appeared on sailing vessels in the fourteenth century, around the same time as their larger brothers, the cannon. (The second type of ring and stave cannon shown on page 153 is a swivel gun.)

Swivel guns are small lightweight cannon mounted on a horseshoe-shaped pivoting mount. This mount ended in a post, which fit into a socket on the railing (similar to an oar-lock on a rowboat). This made it extremely easy to aim. These guns were used mainly to destroy or disable ships.

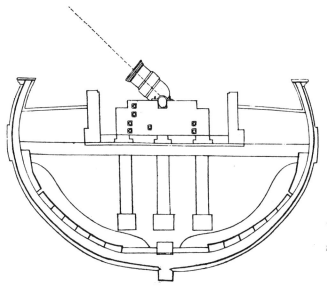

Ship's mortar, showing the additional bracing required for artillary of such massive force.

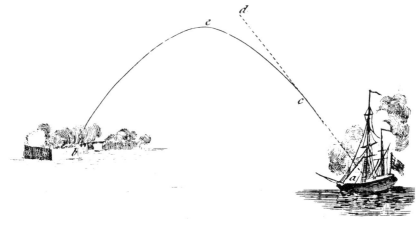

Mortar firing at a fortress

The French fleet demands return of the French consul. The Algerians willingly comply by way of a mortar.

MORTARS

One of the most devastating weapons carried aboard ships wasn't a cannon—it was the mortar. These monsters weighed up to 3 tons or more, and ships had to be specially built to carry them. The tremendous forces these giant guns generated when they fired would have caved in the deck on a regular vessel. These special ships were called "bomb ketches." They were usually named after volcanoes.

Cannons were highly prized aboard pirate vessels, as they were the deadliest weapons of the time. Whenever prizes were taken, one of the first things they took aboard were cannons from the captured vessels. This resulted in a hodgepodge of many different types and sizes. Since accurate firing of these pieces was more art than science at this time, trained cannoneers were highly valued and were often "persuaded" to join the crew.

With their highly mobile vessels and heavy armament, pirate vessels virtually controlled the Caribbean in the mid-seventeenth to early eighteenth centuries. Aye, cannon were a major factor in helping create "The Golden Age of Piracy."

In the heat of battle, with vast clouds of smoke blowing in through the open gun ports, the flash and roar of the cannons, the screams of the wounded, and the sulphurous smell of burning gunpowder, the cramped and overcrowded gun decks must have seemed like hell itself to the valiant gun crews. Ships lived or died depending on the bravery and skill of their gun crews. They were the true heroes of the great age of sail.

Recipes from Gaston's Galley

MAKE YER OWN CANNONBALLS

This easy-to-make no-bake recipe will give you plenty of ammo for your next party or get-together.

You will need:

1 cup creamy or chunky peanut butter
1½ cups powdered milk
1 cup honey
1 teaspoon vanilla
Shredded coconut, optional

In a medium bowl, combine the peanut butter, powdered milk, honey, and vanilla. Roll walnut-sized pieces of dough into balls and set on waxed paper. Refrigerate until firm. Makes 24 to 30 balls.

Optional: roll in shredded coconut before chilling.

PASS THE CANNONBALL

An outside game on a warm day.
Players will get wet!

You'll Need:

† 8 or more balloons per team, preferably black to look
   like cannonballs (have extras ready due to breakage)
† 2 big laundry baskets or cardboard boxes per team

Divide the pirates into two or more crews. The members of each crew should form a long line, with the crewmen standing about 5 feet apart (or more for a greater challenge). At the start of the line, place one basket with all the balloons.

At the end of the line, place an empty basket. When the captain blows the whistle, start tossing the "cannonball" balloons down the line. When one makes it successfully to the end, place it in the basket at the end of the line.

The winning team is the one with the most "cannonballs" in their basket when time is up.

Variations: Use raw eggs instead of water balloons (definitely an outside game).

The Gun Captain

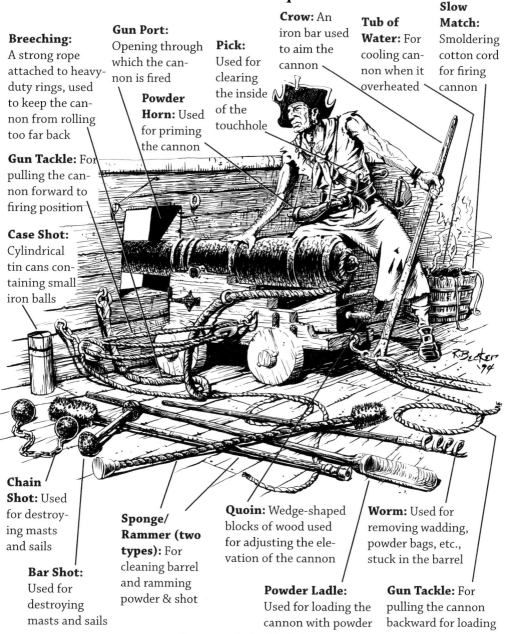

Breeching: A strong rope attached to heavy-duty rings, used to keep the cannon from rolling too far back

Gun Tackle: For pulling the cannon forward to firing position

Case Shot: Cylindrical tin cans containing small iron balls

Gun Port: Opening through which the cannon is fired

Powder Horn: Used for priming the cannon

Pick: Used for clearing the inside of the touchhole

Crow: An iron bar used to aim the cannon

Tub of Water: For cooling cannon when it overheated

Slow Match: Smoldering cotton cord for firing cannon

Chain Shot: Used for destroying masts and sails

Bar Shot: Used for destroying masts and sails

Sponge/ Rammer (two types): For cleaning barrel and ramming powder & shot

Quoin: Wedge-shaped blocks of wood used for adjusting the elevation of the cannon

Powder Ladle: Used for loading the cannon with powder

Worm: Used for removing wadding, powder bags, etc., stuck in the barrel

Gun Tackle: For pulling the cannon backward for loading

(Drawing by Richard Becker)

WHAT TABLE MANNERS?

I f, for just one week, you had to live on the food that sailors ate, you would never again complain about having to eat broccoli. The food aboard ships was probably bad quality to begin with. To save money, shipowners scrimped where they could. Then, after weeks at sea, the food got worse and worse.

MAY YOU NEVER GET WEEVILS IN YER BISCUITS!

Bread did not last for long without getting moldy. Instead, ships brought along barrels of "ship's biscuit" or "hardtack." It was also called "sea biscuit" or "ship's bread," and a whole lot of other names, some not fit to print here. They baked the biscuit twice to make it hard and dry (the drier the biscuit, the less likely it was to get moldy). For really long voyages, they might bake it four times! This biscuit was so hard you could hammer a nail with it. A sailor had to soak a biscuit in water, ale, or other liquid to soften it enough to eat without cracking a tooth.

Not only was the hardtack hard, but soon bugs started living in it. The weevil is a small little beetle that laid its eggs in the hardtack. Soon, little maggots were squirming around, living off of the flour in the biscuit. That is why many sailors ate their food when it was nearly dark so they didn't have to look at the maggots. Some sailors didn't mind too much. The little wrigglers did provide extra protein. Some sailors collected a handful of maggots, then browned them in some fat over a fire, and spread them like paste onto a biscuit (a poor man's peanut butter . . . YUM).

Certain types of cheeses could last a long time without spoiling. The harder the cheese, the longer it lasted. The cheeses were so hard, there are stories of sailors carving buttons out of cheese.

Before a voyage, meat was dried or salted and brought aboard in casks. Dried meat was similar to a very dry and tough jerky. Salt beef, salt pork, and salt fish (and even salt horse) was preserved by soaking it in brine. It was so salty, bugs and bacteria could not live in it. And people could not eat it. The salt had to be removed before cooking by soaking the salted food, then changing the water, and soaking it again. Even so, it was still very salty. Sailors also used hard salt beef to carve buttons.

Sometimes live meat was brought on board (goats, chickens, pigs, even cows were kept aboard; it got pretty stinky). Live animals usually provided meat for the officers. Once in a great while, the sailors might get some fresh meat.

At the start of a voyage, there were fresh vegetables—peas, beans, onions, and turnips. But as the fresh food ran out (or went bad), dried vegetables were used. Dried peas were the most common.

There are many stories of long voyages where food ran short. Here is an example from the explorer Magellan's Pacific crossing: "We ate only old biscuit reduced to powder, and full of grubs, and stinking from the dirt which the rats had made on it when eating the good biscuit, and we drank water that was yellow and stinking. We also ate the ox hides which were under the main yard so that the yard should not break the rigging [the ox hides were used as cushioning] . . . also the sawdust of wood, and rats."

Not only did food run short, many times so did the water. The water or wine casks sprang leaks. Water stored in wooden barrels turned green and became infested with bugs and green slime. Sailors tried to catch rainwater during storms by using buckets and by collecting the runoff from the sails. There were some trips where water ran out and the crew had to drink their own urine to survive.

After all this, I bet that broccoli on your dinner plate is looking better and better.

An Authentic Old Salt's Recipe

TRADITIONAL HARDTACK

Make hardtack with the following recipe and see what it was like to eat what the sailors of old often ate. There's only one ingredient missing—the weevils!

You'll need:

1 cup water (or less)
4 cups flour
Salt to taste

Add only enough water to the flour to make a stiff dough. Roll the dough out on a floured surface about ½ inch thick. Cut it into square pieces about 2½ to 3 inches. Place each piece on a baking sheet. Poke holes in the top with a fork. Bake at 250 degrees F for one hour, or until lightly browned. If you want it to be really authentic, you can bake it a second time. But watch your teeth! It will be really hard.

EAT A LIME

"Y ou scurvy dog!" How many times has a pirate heard this phrase? So what is
scurvy, and how does a "dog" of a sailor get it?

The Elizabethan Sea Dog Richard Hawkins, son of John Hawkins, called
scurvy "the plague of the sea, and the spoil of mariners." He knew it was the cause of
thousands of deaths at sea. But he also knew what helped prevent scurvy: " . . . that
which I have seen most fruitful for this sickness is sour oranges and lemons."

In 1497, Portuguese explorer Vasco da Gama's crew got scurvy. He reported on his
voyage to India that his men "suffered from their gums, which grew over their teeth
so that they could not eat. Their legs also swelled, and other parts of the body, and
these swellings spread until the suffered died, without exhibiting symptoms of any
other disease."

A doctor in the 1600s wrote: "The disease brings with it a great desire to drinke, and
causeth a generall swelling of all parts of the body, especially the legs and gums, and
many times teeth fall out of the jaw without paine."

Scurvy is a terrible disease. It saps your strength. It makes your gums swell and your
teeth fall out. Dark blotches appear on your skin. Your legs swell up, and old wounds
that have been healed for years reopen as if new. Bones get brittle and break easily. If
the disease continues, it gets worse and worse until the sailor dies from it. There are
many reports of ships on long voyages losing large parts of their crew to scurvy.

It took awhile for people to figure out how and why sailors got scurvy. From the
1400s, people knew scurvy had something to do with the lack of fresh fruits and vegetables. They knew eating these could reverse the disease.

Today, we know our bodies need vitamin C and the other vitamins that fresh fruits
and veggies give us. If you don't get these vitamins, strange things begin to happen to
your body. Scurvy is a disease that results from not getting vitamins.

People had not yet learned good ways to keep food fresh for long periods. They did
not have freezers and refrigerators. This was a problem for sailors who went on long
voyages across big oceans without having a chance to get fresh food along the way.

With the poor diet that seamen got in the 1600s and 1700s, symptoms of scurvy
could appear after as little as six weeks at sea.

Vitamin C is fragile. In foods that contain vitamin C, its strength can be weakened
by exposure to heat, sunlight, air, just sitting around for a long time, and contact with
copper (the pots that sea cooks used were usually made of copper).

Human bodies need vitamin C to make collagen, a protein that holds our cells
together, especially scar tissue. When a body runs out of vitamin C, the collagen
begins to come apart. Recent wounds never heal. Then old wounds reopen as scar
tissue breaks down.

Many different recipes to prevent scurvy were tried:

† boiled-down concentrate of lemons called "rob";
  † a powder called "saloop" (made from orchid roots);
    † dried malt;
      † pickled cabbage (sauerkraut).

Of these preventatives, pickled cabbage was one of the few preserved foods that not only had vitamin C in useful amounts but also kept well. In fact, it had long been used among the Dutch.

Once the British figured out the cause of scurvy in the mid 1700s, they then made a practice of carrying limes on ships as much as possible. They mixed a certain amount of limejuice with their rum ration every day. This led to their nickname of "Limeys."

The word "scurvy" originally referred to someone whose skin was covered with scabs (a result of scurvy). The word later came to also mean something or someone that was sorry, worthless, and vile.

Now, the next time yer mother tells you to eat all yer veggies, are ya gonna do it? Otherwise, you might become a "scurvy dog."

Has Ya Got Scurvy?

The 10 Signs of Scurvy

1. Yer fingernails & lips turn bluish.
2. Yer gums are sore & bleed easily.
3. Yer teeth are loose & even start falling out.
4. You lose yer appetite fer rum.
5. Rats drool at the sight of you.
6. You can no longer swing the cat.
7. The bilge water starts ta smell good to you.
8. You can't remember how to find the poop deck.
9. Yer extremities start fallin' off at an alarming rate.
10. Ya swells up, turns purple & they use you for a buoy.

BILGE RAT TARTAR: FINDING FRESH MEAT AT SEA

After several months at sea, the food on board ship was really, REALLY bad. The meat was rotten and wormy, fresh vegetables were long gone, and the salt beef was so hard that they carved buttons out of it. The almost indestructible hardtack biscuits were crumbling to dust. Even the water had turned funny colors and was smelling really foul. But there was one type of meat that was fresh, nutritious, and plentiful on board. We're talking about a nice fat bilge rat.

DRAT! THEY'RE RATS!

This is a game with rats. It is A.S.P.C.A. approved.
You will need:

† String
† Tape
† Bamboo poles, about ½–¾ inch in diameter and about 3 feet long
† Large-diameter rubber bands
† 12–24 plastic rats*
† Stopwatch or timer

This is a fun game for a pirate party. Before your party starts, make "fishing poles" (actually, they are "ratting poles"). Cut a length of string about 3 feet long. With tape, fix one end of the string to the tip of the pole. Tie a rubber band at the other end of the string.

To play the game, pile the rats in a heap on the floor. Make a line on the floor with masking tape. The players must stand behind this line while playing (let little kids stand a little closer). Give the first player a "ratting" pole. The idea is to "hook" a rat around a leg, tail, or whisker with the rubber band and hoist it back over the line.

Give each player 1 minute. See who can catch the most rats in that time.

*Rats can usually be purchased from Oriental Tradering Company, as well as several other sources, especially around Halloween www.oriental trading.com.

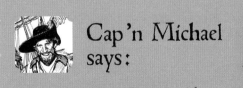

Cap'n Michael says:

Mmmmm . . . Roast Rat on a stick, and you can use the whiskers for dental floss when yer done.

There are many accounts from Royal Navy sailors that tell how they added some fresh meat to their diet. (We imagine a few pirates might have done this too.) They caught rats and fed them pieces of ship's biscuit to fatten them up. When they got nice and fat, the sailor killed the poor little ratties, dredged them in flour, and fried them up. When cooked up, there was even a special name for such a delicacy. They were called "millers," perhaps from the coating of flour.

Seabirds were rarely caught and used for fresh meat (such as noddies or boobies) because they gave such little meat. They were only eaten in an emergency, such as being stranded or adrift at sea. And no matter what, you certainly did not want to kill an albatross. Just talk to the Ancient Mariner to find out about the hazards of that one. (The "Rime of the Ancient Mariner" is the story of a sailor who is cursed for killing an albatross, from a famous poem by Samuel Taylor Coleridge.)

IS THAT A TURTLE I SMELL COOKIN'?

The buccaneers roamed widely through the Caribbean and Spanish Main. Food was usually hit and miss, with periods of feast or famine—often the latter. His diet may not have always been healthy, but the typical buccaneer ate much better than the salt pork and maggoty biscuit diet that was on hand aboard naval and merchant ships.

Buccaneers didn't have to depend on the supplies that the Admiralty Board or some shipping company decided they could live on. They controlled provisioning of their vessels. No more half rotten food if they could help it. They liked their food fresh and they knew how to get it from the islands.

Buccaneers often put in at secluded

Buccaneers would often go well out of their way to visit an island where sea turtles came ashore. Upside-down, turtles could be kept alive aboard ship for long periods of time, thus providing a source of fresh meat. This delicacy was so popular, some turtle species were almost driven into extinction.

bays for water or food. Sometimes they stayed longer to careen their ships. While some of the crew worked on the ship, hunting parties looked for food. As luck had it, food flourished on the islands. Native fruits and vegetables grew in profusion. There were yams, bananas (plantains), pineapples, papayas, guavas, dates, and other fruits. Those huge, green bananas—plantains—were found to be useful on ship. They did not ripen

Buccaneers fishing for turtles.

and spoil but remained hard. Yet, thrown into hot ashes, they baked into a tasty and healthy treat.

Buccaneers often hunted the cattle and wild boar that roamed wild on the islands. From the local Arawak Indians, they had learned how to smoke the meat on a wood rack. This process was called "boucaning," which lent its name to the word *boucanier* (French for buccaneer).

Buccaneers also cooked young pigs luau-style. They built a deep fire pit to roast them. Seasoned with some stolen spices and wrapped with the large banana leaves, the little piglet emerged tasty and tender. (See the Jerk Pork recipe on page 170.)

Banana leaves were also used to cook fish. The sea gave up a wide variety of food. Many shellfish were found close to shore, and they found their way into much of the pirates' cooking. With local greens added along with the juice of some lemons or limes, some quite tasty dishes could be prepared.

The resourceful seamen were quick to put the abundance of the Caribbean to their use. Much of today's Caribbean cuisine came from buccaneer cooking. Local tubers with wild garlic and onion mixed with a potpourri of fish and spices were the forerunner of gumbo. And the buccaneers' favorite concoction (when there were enough ingredients

An Authentic Old Salt's Recipe

JERK PORK:
COOKING A SUCKLING PIG MAROON-STYLE

Start with a freshly butchered suckling pig. Season it inside and out with salt, pepper, and allspice (the dark brown berry of a tree growing in Jamaica). Stuff the inside of the pig with cooked rice mixed with a little ginger and chopped onion. Wrap the entire pig in pimento leaves for flavor and green banana leaves for protection.

To prepare the cooking pit, dig a hole about two feet deep, line it with rocks, and build a wood fire in it (have an adult help you with the fire). When the fire has burned down to the coals, remove any chunks of unburnt wood and place the leaf-wrapped pig in the hole. Using a shovel, rake the coals toward the pig so it is surrounded on all sides (including the top) by live coals and hot rocks. The hole is then covered with a piece of corrugated metal, and dirt is put on top of that.

When the pig is cooked in three or four hours, it is unwrapped and browned over hot coals or in the oven. Heavenly!

at hand) was a type of stew called "salmagundi."

Salmagundi consisted of marinated meat (often turtle, fish, pork, chicken, or beef) mixed with any type of vegetable (cabbage and onions were common), eggs, anchovies, pickled herring, grapes, limes, wine or ale, garlic, salt, pepper, oil, and spices (whatever was on hand). The meats was roasted, chopped into chunks, and marinated in the spiced wine or ale. The meat was then combined with whatever other foods they had, and all was highly seasoned with salt, pepper, garlic, and mustard seed, and covered with oil and vinegar. Also called "grand salad," its name probably derived from a warping of the medieval French word *salemine*, meaning salted or highly seasoned.

The assorted backgrounds of the buccaneers, and a knack for making something different out of simple things, lent adventure to meals. No matter how it turned out, buccaneers were sure glad they weren't eating hardtack and weevils anymore.

Pastimes for Scurvy Dogs

BELLY TIMBER:
HOW DO YOU FEED A CREW OF HUNGRY PIRATES?

If you are throwing a pirate party, you can have a lot of fun coming up with great "pirate" food for it. Make up ghastly pirate names for any food or drink you serve, like Monkey's Blood Punch or Shark Gristle Cake. Decorate the cake with Treasure Island decorations. Lego pirate toys and other small plastic pirates make great cake decorations. Make skull 'n' crossbones cookies out of sugar cookie dough using a pirate-shaped cookie cutter.

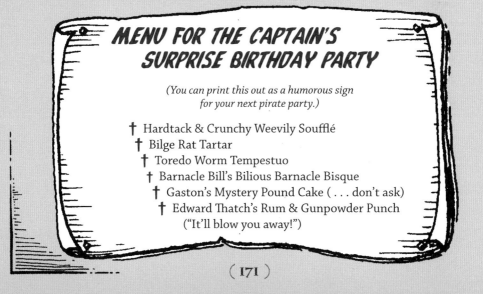

MENU FOR THE CAPTAIN'S SURPRISE BIRTHDAY PARTY

(You can print this out as a humorous sign for your next pirate party.)

† Hardtack & Crunchy Weevily Soufflé
† Bilge Rat Tartar
† Toredo Worm Tempestuo
† Barnacle Bill's Bilious Barnacle Bisque
† Gaston's Mystery Pound Cake (. . . don't ask)
† Edward Thatch's Rum & Gunpowder Punch
("It'll blow you away!")

WATERMELON PIRATE SHIP

A watermelon fruit bowl shaped like a ship, with cucumber long boats. You will need:

1 large, long watermelon
Carving knife or special rind decoration (pumpkin carving) tool
Paper
Markers to make designs on sails
Wooden skewers
Tape
String
Fruit salad (oranges, pineapple, strawberries, cantaloupe are suggested)
Cucumbers or zucchini (optional)
Toothpicks (optional)

Directions:

1. Cut a thin slice lengthwise from the bottom of the watermelon to make a flat base so the melon won't rock. (Don't rock the boat!)

2. Using a picture of a pirate ship as a guide, draw the outlines for the ship.

3. Use a knife or decorating tool to cut along the lines of the pattern (you might need adult help for this part). Cut all the way through the rind.

4. Remove the top section of rind; you may have to cut it into two pieces and remove one piece at a time. Reserve for later.

5. Remove the red watermelon flesh and place in a large bowl.

6. Use paper to make the sails. You can write a message on the largest sail. ("Happy Birthday," "Congratulations," etc.)

7. Use long wooden skewers as masts to hold up the sails. Attach sideways wooden skewers to the top and bottom of each paper sail. These are your yardarms. Tape the yardarms to your masts.

8. Add more detail to your ship, such as placing gun ports on the side and carving the name of the ship across the back.

9. Be creative and use the unused top portion of the rind to make other parts of the ship, such as the ship's wheel, gangplank, and cannons.

10. In the large bowl, mix the reserved watermelon with the other fruit salad. Fill the open part of the ship with fruit salad mixture.

11. Add finishing touches to your boat. Use string to make shrouds and rat-lines on the side. More string can make the various lines on a ship.

12. Don't forget a black pirate flag at the topmast!

13. Use cucumbers (or zucchini) to make long boats to accompany the pirate ship. Toothpicks can be the oars. You can put Lego pirates or small plastic pirate toys in the long boats and on the pirate ship for an extra touch. Use another skewer with a piece of paper to add smaller sails to the cucumber boats.

I'M JUST IN IT FOR THE RUM

Now, you've all heard the stories about how much pirates liked to drink. Aye, those rum-sodden sailors were supposed to be legendary in that regard. Many books, movies, and stories show them this way. Pirates have been shown as being excessively drunk most of the time.

Only problem with this idea was that in the 1600s and 1700s, almost EVERYONE drank alcohol, and lots of it—EVEN SMALL CHILDREN. (Now don't you kids go sayin' that Cap'n Michael and Jamaica Rose told you it was okay to drink, cuz it's not. It's not good for yer growing brain cells. But kids of those times had little choice. Read on, we'll explain.)

Water was often unhealthy. Near towns and farms, water sources frequently got polluted with waste from people and livestock. Drinking the water could often make you sick. Many people, especially kids, got sick and died from drinking bad water. Scientists were only just learning about germs and bacteria and very small things that make water impure. People found it was much safer to glug down beer, wine, or even stronger drink, than to drink the water. Alcohol kills off germs (similar to how it destroys your brain cells!). People found it safer to drink beer or wine than to take a chance on the water. It was better to be healthy, alive, and have your thinking be a little fuzzy than risk staying sober while drinking water.

The water situation was even worse onboard ships. Water was stored in wooden kegs for weeks and months at a time. Can you imagine how putrid already questionable water became when stored in wooden kegs for a long time? It turned GREEN and slimy, and would get wormy things wiggling in it. YUCK!

Ships often made stops just to get fresh water, but when crossing big oceans, it could be a long way before the next landfall. Water often went bad.

Instant Pirate . . . Just Add Rum

On the other hand, beer, rum, and other fermented drinks kept nicely in wooden barrels. After a time, wine might turn more vinegary and beer could get a sour taste, but they didn't get putrid and unhealthy. Now rum, on the other hand, just got better and better the longer it stayed in an oak keg.

Sailors on naval ships and merchant ships usually got a liquor ration twice a day. There were actually several benefits to drinking alcohol:

† It provided liquid calories.
  † It provided a sense of warmth and strengthened the sailors against the wet and cold.
    † Hardships could be temporarily forgotten in a drunken haze.
      † It helped promote brotherhood and friendship among the crew
        † Boredom brought on by days of empty ocean could be relieved.
          † In the face of battle, it could give you a sense of courage. Liquor was even called "Dutch Courage" because of the practice of the Dutch in handing around drinks to their crews just before battle.

Pirates had one more benefit to drinking:

† Freedom to drink at any time was definite proof to a pirate that he was free—a symbol of personal liberty. Onboard a British navy ship, a sailor only got a small ration of rum, once a day, and onboard most merchant vessels, the crew wasn't allowed to drink at all.

When the sailors and pirates got to shore, the drinking continued. In Port Royal, with a population of three thousand in 1680, there were one hundred licensed taverns and grogshops. Who knows how many unlicensed ones there were.

Drinking and carousing sometimes caused disastrous results for pirate crews. Drink led to the end of Blackbeard. He and his crew stayed up late partying and drinking "punch" with Samuel Odell, a merchant friend who happened along in his vessel the day before. The next morning, as the pirate crew lay around in a drunken fog, Lieutenant Robert Maynard was able to overcome Blackbeard and his crew.

Bartholomew Roberts was killed and his crew captured as they lay about their ships in a drunken stupor after a night celebrating a successful attack. This was ironic because Bartholomew Roberts was well known as a teetotaler (he avoided strong drink and sipped tea instead). He even tried to control the drinking of his crew. His pirate articles restricted drinking to the main deck only. This was for fear of fire and to reduce fighting in the close quarters of belowdecks. Overall, he was one of the most successful pirates, having captured more than four hundred vessels, and perhaps his lack of drinking contributed to his success. But he couldn't completely stop his men from drinking, and that was their eventual downfall.

B.Y.O.L.:
BRING YOUR OWN LIME

Did the pirates drink only rum? Of course not, mates! They drank whatever they could get their hands on. Rum was the most common liquor available. If they had a choice, though, they preferred brandy. Wine was usually drunk if nothing else was available, though the French buccaneers were partial to it (and it was useful in that it protected against scurvy).

"A hott, hellish & terrible liquor" is what sailors first called rum. The English called it "rumbullion," which was soon shortened to rum. It was also called "kill-devil." In 1707, Dr. Hans Sloane (Henry Morgan's doctor) wrote that "rum is well-called Kill-Devil, for perhaps no year passes without it having killed more than a thousand." Henry Morgan's death in 1688 was probably caused in good part by his overdrinking.

Rum became available in the Caribbean during the 1640s. It was distilled from molasses (a by-product of the new sugar cane industry). Molasses and the skimmings from the boiling sugar kettles fermented naturally. It was then distilled to result in a clear liquor. It darkened as it aged in wooden casks. Rum was as common and as cheap as beer is today.

The buccaneers mixed rum with wine, tea, limejuice, sugar, and spices. They called this "punch." The number and variety of ingredients varied greatly. As it took some effort to make, punch was usually made at parties. They served it in a big bowl, either hot or cold, and the revelers often drank it straight from the dipper. In 1689, the day after Christmas, Captain William Kidd met with another captain in a tavern. They had a punch with the following recipe: "Rum, Water, Lime-Juice, Egg yolk, Sugar with a little nutmeg scrap'd on top." (Pirates weren't alone in enjoying punch; it was the most popular beverage in colonial America.)

The term "grog" was not used until 1740, when Admiral Edward Vernon ordered the sailors' rum ration be mixed with tea (or water) and limejuice. The tea diluted the rum, and the limejuice prevented scurvy. At sea, Vernon wore a cloak made of grogram wool, and thus earned his nickname "Old Grogram." The watered-down rum was thus named "grog" in his honor.

Aye, pirates loved to drink and were very creative in the types of drinks they produced. But most never learned moderation, which was the downfall of many a pirate at the end.

IT'LL BLOW YOU AWAY

Captain Jack Sparrow wasn't the only pirate who worried about the rum being gone. Blackbeard's crew got very cranky when their rum was gone. Captain Blackbeard wrote in his ship's logbook:

"Such a day; rum all out. Our company somewhat sober; a [darned] confusion amongst us! Rogues a plotting. Talk of separation. So I looked sharp for a prize [and] took one with a great deal of liquor aboard. So kept the company hot, [darned] hot, then all things went well again."

Blackbeard had a special recipe for rum punch. The secret ingredient was gunpowder! He would add the gunpowder as the last step in making the punch. When it was set on fire, the punch sizzled, flamed up, and popped. Quite an exciting drink!

And now you can serve Blackbeard's famous punch to your pirate crew:

Punch Bowl

Recipes from Gaston's Galley

LIMEADE GROG

(nonalcoholic)

You will need:

2 (12-ounce) cans frozen limeade concentrate
2 (12-ounce) cans frozen lemonade concentrate
2 (2-liter) bottles lemon-lime soda
1 (2-liter) bottle ginger ale
2 quarts lime sherbet, in chunks

Combine liquids in a large punch bowl. Mix in the lime sherbet just before serving, letting the chunks of sherbet float on top.

BLACKBEARD'S "GUNPOWDER AND RUM" PUNCH

(nonalcoholic)

¼ pound green tea leaves (it will be a lot cheaper and easier if you buy the loose leaves in bulk, not tea bags)

2 quarts cold water

3 cups orange juice (instead of brandy)

2 cups lime (or lemon) juice

1 cup firmly packed light brown sugar

3 quarts ginger ale or ginger beer (nonalcoholic; instead of rum)

1 cup drained maraschino cherries

1 (20-ounce) can crushed pineapple, including the juice

Pop Rocks* (instead of gunpowder)

Pour the tea and water into a sun tea jar and let it sit outside most of the day. Strain out the tea leaves. Add the juices and sugar. Cover and store in the fridge for a couple of days, the longer the better.

The day before your party, make an ice ring. Use 1 quart of the ginger ale for the ice ring. Pour enough ginger ale into a ring mold (or Bundt cake pan) to a depth of ¾ inch. Freeze solid. Then arrange maraschino cherries onto the frozen layer. Carefully pour in another ¼ inch of ginger ale and freeze again to hold the cherries in place. After the cherry mixture is frozen, carefully pour the remaining ginger ale on top. Freeze until ready to use.

Just before you serve the punch to your unsuspecting crewmates, pour the tea/juice mixture into a large punch bowl.

To unmold the ice ring, dip it into a bowl of warm water. When it is loosened, place the ice ring carefully in the chilled punch (you don't want to slosh it).

Add the remaining ginger ale and the pineapple. Invite your fellow pirates over, and then sprinkle your Pop Rocks "gunpowder" on top and let them enjoy the "fireworks."

*Pop Rocks can be ordered through www.poprockscandy.com. If you can't use Pop Rocks, substitute 1 teaspoon black pepper as your gunpowder (but you won't get the "fireworks").

[Special thanks to Cap'n Lane for the Pop Rocks idea.]

"YO-HO-HO AND A BOTTLE OF RUM!"

SHIVER ME TIMBRES!

SOME PIRATES LIKE TO FIDDLE AROUND

"Come give us a jig!" the pirates would often call to the fiddler or piper. They loved singing and dancing to a hornpipe or jig. Lucky was the pirate ship with a musician or two aboard. Especially fortunate were those with an entire band or orchestra, for music helped while away the tedious hours.

Musicians were popular with pirate crews. Musicians, along with doctors, were the only landsmen welcomed aboard ship. Captured musicians were often forced to join pirate crews, thus they were often believed at trials when they claimed to be innocent of piracy.

Though excused from most taxing shipboard duties, musicians were on call any time of the day or night with one exception: "The musicians to have rest on the Sabbath Day [Sunday], but the other six Days & Nights none without special Favour. "(As seen in Bartholomew Roberts' articles.)

Playing the fiddle or flute made a man very popular. The other pirates liked to have him around. Impromptu serenades kept the crew happy. They would sing themselves hoarse while banging out the beat on or with anything handy—barrels, tankards, pots, etc.

Besides merrymaking, musicians had another important role. During battle, they played nautical tunes and drummed out war beats to fire up the crew. The resulting noise and ruckus was called "vaporing." It put dread into the hearts of the crew they were about to attack.

COME, ME YOUNG SAILORS, AND I'LL SING YE A SONG

Pirates of old loved music. Their music may not have been cultured music, but 'twas usually something they could sing or dance to. Pirates, and sailors in general, loved to sing.

Sailors sung two main types of songs aboard ship: work songs and songs for entertainment. The work songs were called shanties. The songs of leisure were called forebitters or fo'c'sle songs.

SHANTIES

A shanty (also spelled "chanty" or "chantey") was always linked with work. They were used to help the sailors work together and all pull at the same time. They also made the work a little less unpleasant.

The earliest proper shanty we know of was written down in 1549. But even in ancient times, sailors sang at their work, when rowing in a galley, or heavin' and haulin'. It's just natural. Many of these "songs" would be more correctly termed a "sing-out." A sing-out is a wild yell given when hauling a rope hand-over-hand, a sort of seed of a shanty. "Heave ho" is a good example.

Most shanties we know about first appeared between 1830 and 1860, mostly aboard the merchant ships. Merchant ships carried the smallest crew possible to save money. It was important to get the men to work together on a small crew. Shanties were great for this.

Shanties usually follow a pattern: a short solo verse sung by the shantyman (the song leader) followed by a lusty chorus that everyone sang.

There were two main types of shanties: the capstan shanty and the halyard shanty.

Capstans were used for raising large heavy objects such as anchors and huge mainyards (the spar hanging from the mainmast). For this, the crew had to walk around and around and around the capstan, pushing at the bars (sort of like pushing a playground merry-go-round). This was heavy work, but the shantyman made it a lot easier by helping everybody walk in step together. Besides, the work was more enjoyable if there was music to go with it.

Halyard comes from "haul yard." Halyard shanties were used as the sailors pulled on a line to raise a heavy yard, or pole. In singing a halyard shanty, the accent was placed on certain words or notes, letting the men know when they should all pull on the line.

Shanties have many variations, often depending on where they came from or honoring certain events. They usually started with a certain set of verses, but a good shantyman could improvise enough verses to continue the song until the work was completed. Shantymen loved to improvise. They often personalized the songs for their own ship, with verses about their captain, officers, and fellow crewman. So you might hear versions of the shanty different than the one you know. Don't worry about it. It's just the result of some shantyman being creative. You might try your own hand at writing a new version of a shanty!

These songs would often be quite dirty with lots of bad words. Sailors LOVED singing dirty songs, especially when the captain wasn't listening. When you see them written in books, they have been cleaned up, replacing the bad words with nicer words and leaving out whole verses if needed.

FO'C'S'LE SONGS

When men were not on duty, they hung around in the crew's quarters (the forecastle, or fo'c'sle). If the weather was nice, they would be out on deck at the fo'c'sle-head. They sang songs for entertainment, called fo'c'sle songs. The fiddles and fifes would emerge especially during the second dogwatch (6–8 p.m.). The sailors would gather around one of the hatches, or on the forecastle head, dancing jigs and hornpipes, and singing. Often they sang songs of farewell, famous (and not-so-famous) vessels, battles at sea, piracy, adventures ashore, their wives and sweethearts, complaints about conditions on board, and sentimental songs of home and family.

SHORE SONGS AND BALLADS

So-called "sailor songs" were written and sung by landsmen. They were the "recruiting posters" of the day. They told of the glories and delights of life at sea. Real sailors knew this was a bunch of garbage. Sailors did not sing these songs. "Sailing, Sailing, over the Bounding Main," now sung by children, was one such song.

In the 1600s and 1700s, professional ballad writers were the news reporters of the day. Exciting news, such as a major sea battle or pirate attack, would be written up as a ballad. They printed the ballads on a single sheet of paper. Small kids sold them on the street as "one-sheets" or "penny ballads" (sold for a penny). Many songs about pirates were written as ballads. The facts were often changed to tell a better story or point out a moral. The famous "Captain Kidd" ballad is a good example.

Remember, pirates were sailors, and they sang the songs of the sea. Singing as one helped them feel like a brotherhood and helped cement them together as a crew. The shanties promoted comradeship and teamwork. It made them feel like they were part of something bigger than themselves. Get a bunch of your mates together, and try singing some of the songs. You'll see what we mean.

HOW DO YA PUT FIFTEEN MEN ON A DEAD MAN'S CHEST?
FROM THE FILES OF CAP'N MICHAEL

Fifteen men on the Dead Man's Chest—
Yo-ho-ho and a bottle of rum!
Drink and the devil had done for the rest—
Yo-ho-ho and a bottle of rum!

The drunken old sailor Billy Bones sings this refrain in the opening pages of one of the most famous pirate novels of all time, *Treasure Island*. What did author Robert Louis Stevenson mean by "Fifteen men on the Dead Man's Chest"? Was there a dog pile of people lying' on some poor dead shipmate's torso? If so, no wonder he died. Having fifteen people on top of you would tend to crush ya a bit (sounds like a game of football gone bad). Or maybe it's fifteen men fighting over their dead mate's sea chest? Does it have anything to do with the chest Captain Jack Sparrow tries to get away from Davy Jones? So, ya might be wondering, "Just what is this chest?"

Fifteen Men on a Dead Man's Chest

Fif - teen men on the Dead Man's Chest, Yo ho ho and a bot - tle of rum,

Drink and the De - vil had done for the rest, Yo ho ho and a bot - tle of rum. The

mate was fixed by the bo-sun's pike. The bo-sun brained with a marlin spike, & Cookies throat wa

marked be like. It had been gripped by fin-gers ten and there they lay all good dead men like

break o' day in a booz-ing ken---- Yo ho ho and a bot-tle of rum!

It turns out, it ain't none of the above. It is actually the name of a place.

There is an island by the name of Dead Man's Chest in the Virgin Islands. Charles Kingsley, an old friend of Robert Louis Stevenson, had taken a trip to the Caribbean and mentioned the island in his book *At Last: A Christmas in the West Indies*. This gave Stevenson the idea to write the bit of song for *Treasure Island*.

Ya can still find that island today. Now it's called Dead Chest Island, near Peter Island in the British Virgin Islands (some may dissent with me, but I say it be true!). It's a barren rocky island with no fresh water. About the only thing alive on it are pelicans and snakes. Local stories tell how the famous Blackbeard stranded fifteen of his crew on Dead Chest Island to punish them. He left only one bottle o' rum with them and nothin' else. They had little chance o' survival. Two of them tried swimming to nearby Peter Island, but they didn't make it. Their bodies washed up on the shore of a fine-looking bay on the island. The local natives call it Deadman's Bay (sounds picturesque, don't ya think?).

Some people will tell ya nearby Norman Island was the model for *Treasure Island*. And wouldn't you know, this island is named for Captain Norman, a pirate himself.

Now, Stevenson didn't write the whole song. He only wrote the four lines of refrain given on page 183, and that was back in 1881.

Ten years later, a journalist named Young Ewing Allison wrote a song to go with those four lines. It was for a musical version of *Treasure Island*. He called his song "The Derelict," but now most people call it by the first line of the refrain, "Fifteen Men on the Dead Man's Chest." It's also called "Bottle of Rum," "Fifteen Men," or "Dead Man's Chest."

There are many versions of the song, because Allison kept tinkering with it and changing it. Other people often sing it their own way, either because they can't remember it all or just don't understand all the words. The version below is the one WE learned and have probably heard most often.

"The Derelict" tells the story of a treasure-filled Spanish galleon captured by pirates. Fighting over how to divvy up the riches, the pirates started killin' each other. Pretty soon they were all dead. With no one at the helm, the ship ran aground at Dead Man's Chest.

The wrecked ship (derelict) waited with her gruesome cargo, until one day another crew discovered it. The song below describes what this new crew saw as they hauled themselves over the railing of the derelict.

Fifteen men on the Dead Man's Chest—
Yo-ho-ho and a bottle of rum!
Drink and the devil had done for the rest—
Yo-ho-ho and a bottle of rum!

"Heave-ho" or "Yo-heave-ho" is a chant sailor's use when pulling heavy things up with ropes, such as raising up a heavy sail. Stevenson changed it a little for his refrain to "Yo-ho-ho." He really started something with those six little letters. The bottle of rum reminds us how the pirates were often drunk. In this case, their drinking led to their fighting and their deaths.

> The mate was fixed by the bo'sun's pike
> And the bo'sun brained with a marlin-spike,
> The cookie's throat was marked belike
> Yo-ho-ho and a bottle of rum!
> It had been clutched by fingers ten.
> And there they lay, all good dead men,
> Like break o' day in a boozin' ken
> Yo-ho-ho and a bottle of rum!

A pike (or boarding pike) was a long spear used on ships (see page 85). The bos'un (short for boatswain, a middle-rank officer) must have stabbed the mate (another officer) with it and pinned him to the wooden deck.

A marlinspike is a wood or metal tool with a pointy end. Lookin' rather like a giant-sized sewing needle. They are usually 6–12 inches long, but can be up to 24 inches long. Sailors use 'em for repairing the ship's rigging, but they would be quite handy fer bashing someone's head.

Cookie is a nickname for the ship's cook. His throat shows bruises from being strangled (considerin' the horrible slop most cooks served, he probably deserved it).

A boozing ken is a bar or tavern, a place where you get booze (liquor). After a night full of drinking, the drunks who are still at the bar will be lying around like dead bodies.

> Fifteen men of the whole ship's list,
> Yo-ho-ho and a bottle of rum!
> Dead and bedamned and their souls gone whist
> Yo-ho-ho and a bottle of rum!

There are fifteen men on the ship's roster. Because of their ill deeds, they are now cursed, and their souls have not gone to Heaven.

> The skipper lay with his nob in gore
> Where the scullion's axe his cheek had shore,
> And the scullion he was stabbed times four
> Yo-ho-ho and a bottle of rum!
> And there he lay, and the soggy skies
> Dripped all day long in up-staring eyes
> At murk sunset and at foul sunrise—
> Yo-ho-ho and a bottle of rum!

The captain's head (nob) lays in a pool of blood (gore) from where the cook's assistant (the scullion) attacked him. Someone else stabbed the scullion four times. From sunset to sunrise, the scullion's body lay on the deck, starring up into the heavens as the foul murky weather dripped rain into his sightless eyes.

> Fifteen men of 'em stiff and stark,
> Yo-ho-ho and a bottle of rum!
> Ten of the crew bore the murder mark,
> Yo-ho-ho and a bottle of rum!

Bodies do tend ta' get a bit stiff after lying around for a bit (rigor mortis, ya know).

Accordin' to this song, ten of this crew have been branded as murderers! They were not nice guys. And now they have murdered each other. They used to brand criminals with a hot iron on their cheek or the back of their hand (just like cattle in the Old West). It was a criminal record you couldn't easily hide. "T" was used for "Thief." "P" was for "Pirate" (just like on Jack Sparrow's wrist.) Aye, the British East India Company branded what pirates it didn't hang. The letter "M" was used as a brand, but it did NOT stand for "Murderer." It stood for "Malefactor" (wrongdoer). Murderers would have been hanged if caught. They wouldn't have bothered to brand them first. It is possible, however, criminals might o' given themselves a tattoo or a brand to brag about having murdered someone (similar to gang tattoos nowadays). It would add to their dangerous reputation.

> 'Twas a cutlass swipe or an ounce of lead,
> Or a yawing hole in a battered head,
> And the scuppers glut with a rotting red.
> Yo-ho-ho and a bottle of rum!
> And there they lay, aye, damn my eyes,
> Their lookouts clapped on Paradise,
> And souls bound just contrariwise—
> Yo-ho-ho and a bottle of rum!

Now, was it a slash from a sword, or a bullet hole (ounce of lead), or a bashed-in head that killed 'em? Whatever it was, it looks ta me like they all met their fate right there on the deck. There was a lot of blood running out of the drainholes (scuppers) and down the outside of the ship. The dead men's eyes (lookouts) looked up to Heaven (Paradise), but their souls were going the other way.

> Fifteen men of 'em good and true,
> Yo-ho-ho and a bottle of rum!
> Every man jack could 'a sailed with Old Pew
> Yo-ho-ho and a bottle of rum!

If these men had been so "good and true," they wouldn't all be dead now, would they? But I suppose this means they had been thought to be good sailors (when not drunk and fighting with everyone else). Jack was a term for a sailor in general. In *Treasure Island*, Blind Pew is the one who gives the Black Spot to Billy Bones. Perhaps before he was blinded, he was simply known as Old Pew.

> There was chest on chest of Spanish gold,
> And a ton of plate in the middle hold,
> And the cabins riot with loot untold—
> Yo-ho-ho and a bottle of rum!
> And there they lay that had took the plum,
> With a sightless glare and their lips struck dumb,
> While we shared all by rule o' thumb—
> Yo-ho-ho and a bottle of rum!

This part is about the fine riches they captured from the Spanish. Chests piled on top of other chests, and all full of Spanish gold. Aye, seems clear enough—a vast treasure of golden doubloons and bars of gold.

A ton of plate didn't mean they had a hold full o' fine china. *Plata* is Spanish for "silver." English pirates called it plate. And there was a TON of it in the hold (where ya keep the cargo). More loot was found in the cabin. Probably the captain kept the best stuff in his room. "Took the plum"—remember Little Jack Horner who pulled out a plum? It means they caught a big, rich prize.

Now the pirates are all dead, with eyes staring, and mouths quiet. If they had just worked together and shared everything equally, they wouldn't all be dead.

> More was seen through the sternlight screen,
> Yo-ho-ho and a bottle of rum!
> Chartings no doubt where the woman had been,
> Yo-ho-ho and a bottle of rum!

A sternlight was a light on the back of the ship, like a taillight. Looking through its screen, traces of a woman were spotted. Had she been a passenger on the Spanish galleon? Or someone's maid?

> A flimsy shift on a bunker cot
> With a dirk slit sheer through the bosom spot
> And the lace stiff dry in a purplish blot—
> Yo-ho-ho and a bottle of rum!

Oh was she wench or some shudderin' maid
That dared the knife and took the blade
By God! she had stuff for a plucky jade
Yo-ho-ho and a bottle of rum!

Her thin dress is found on one of the beds. Appears ta me she was stabbed in the heart. They saw the slit made by the dirk (a thin-bladed dagger) with dried blood staining the lace all around it. Looks like the poor lass that was wearing it came to a bad end.

Who was she? A highborn lady or a maidservant? Did she stab herself so the pirates couldn't hurt her? Ya can tell the narrator admires her courage. He calls her a "plucky jade" (feisty woman), though "jade" is usually not a nice word for a woman (but in this case it rhymed with "blade").

Fifteen men on the Dead Man's Chest,
Yo-ho-ho and a bottle of rum!
Drink and the Devil had done for the rest,
Yo-ho-ho and a bottle of rum!

We wrapped 'em all in a mainsail tight,
With twice ten turns of a hawser's bight.
And we heaved 'em over and out of sight,
Yo-ho-ho and a bottle of rum!
With a yo-heave-ho and a fare-ye-well,
And a sullen plunge in the sullen swell.
Ten fathoms deep on the road to hell—
Yo-ho-ho and a bottle of rum!

The men who found the derelict decided ta give the dead crew a proper burial at sea. They rolled the bodies up using the canvas from the largest sail. A hawser is a large rope used fer tying a ship up at the docks. A bight is a loop in the rope. They looped the hawser twenty times around the bodies as they wrapped 'em for burial.

Chanting "yo-heave-ho" as they picked up the weight of the bodies, they threw 'em over into the sea, with a few words of farewell. The bundled bodies sank down to the bottom, 60 feet below (one fathom = 6 feet).

Obviously, these lads were not heaven-bound.

PIRATED RIDDLES

irates love a good laugh as well as a good tune. You can amaze and amuse yer friends with some fun seagoing riddles. Here are some of our favorites:

THE CLASSICS

How much did the pirate pay to have his ears pierced?

A buck an ear.

What does a pirate keep under his buckin' hat?

His buckin' ears.

What type of socks do pirates wear?

Arrrrgyle.

PIRATE ILLITERACY

What's a pirate's favorite letter of the alphabet?

Arrrr!

But what's really a pirate's favorite letter?

P! Because it's like an R, but it's missing a leg!

Why does it take pirates so long to learn the alphabet?

Because they can spend years at C!

So how did the pirate finally learn how to read?

With "Hooked" on phonics!

What does a dyslexic pirate say?

RRAAAAAAAAAAA!

What else does a dyslexic pirate say?

Oy oh oh!

What do you call a stupid pirate?

The pillage idiot!

What do you get when you cross a pirate with a librarian?

Cap'n Book!

GIMPY PIRATES

Why is pirating addictive?

They say once ye lose yer first hand, ye get hooked!

What do you call a pirate with two eyes and two legs?

Rookie!

What do you call a woman with only one leg?

Eileen.

How do you keep a peg-leg pirate from robbing your house?

Fill your lawn with beavers!

What is a common injury pirates get from walking the plank in bare feet?

Long John Sliver.

What's Captain Hook's favorite store?

The Secondhand Shop!

What has 8 legs, 8 arms, and 8 eyes?

8 pirates.

What goes thump-thump Arr!, thump-thump Arr!?

A pirate falling down the stairs!

AN OCEAN OF ADVENTURE

What lies at the bottom of the ocean and twitches?

A nervous wreck!

Why do sharks only swim in salt water?

Because pepper water makes them sneeze.

Where is the ocean the deepest?

On the bottom.

What do you call a neurotic octopus?

A crazy mixed-up squid.

What lies on the bottom of the ocean and shoots people?

Billy the Squid.

What's got fins . . . and an arm?

A happy shark.

What do sea monsters love to eat?

Fish and ships.

Why did Blackbeard give his ship a coat of paint?

The timbers were shivering.

What sort of gas mileage does Cap'n Kidd get out of his warship?

He gets 35 miles to the galleon!

PARROTS AND OTHER CRITTERS

What has fur, four legs, and flies?

A dead bilge rat.

What's a pirate's favorite animal?

The aaarrrrrdvaaarrrk.

There are five parrots sitting in a tree. If you shoot one, how many would be left?

None, the others would have flown off.

JUST SAY ARRRRR

While playing poker, what did the captain say to his first mate when he spilled rum all over the cards?

Arrrrgh, matey, swab the deck!!!!

Why couldn't the pirates play cards?

The captain was standing on the deck!

What do pirates use to blow their noses?

Anchor-chiefs.

Why do pirates always carry a bar of soap?

So if they're shipwrecked they can wash themselves to shore.

What do you get when you cross a pirate with a zucchini?

A Squashbuckler!!!

What are pirates a part of?

Avast conspiracy!

What do you call pirate vomit?

Pieces he ate.

Where did the pirate learn to draw his sword?

At the arrrrt institute.

What is a pirate's least favorite color?

Maroon!

Where do pirates keep their bathrooms?

On the poop deck!

What's a pirate's favorite kind of cookie?

Ships Ahoy.

Where do pirates store their gym clothes?

Davy Jones' locker.

RATTLE ME BONES!

GAMES PIRATES PLAYED

The ship has just made port after a successful venture "on the account," and the booty has just been divvied up. Does the average buccaneer sock away his money to save up for that plantation he's had his heart set on? Nay! Most of them eagerly set out to spend all their money on drink, women, and gambling.

Sailors in general loved to game and gamble. It was as popular as drinking. Among common sailors, games with cards and dice were the most popular, with much gambling on the results.

Other games included tables (a gambling form of backgammon), checkers, and an early version of cribbage without the crib. Twenty-eight lead gaming pieces were found from the shipwreck of the *Whydah*.

Pirates whiled away long hours at sea by gambling. This often lead to accusations of cheating, which then turned to quarrels and fighting. Wise pirate captains, such as Bartholomew Roberts, put anti-gambling and anti-cheating clauses in their ship's articles. Some banned any type of gaming with cards or dice for money. Others limited gambling to only the top deck, hoping to prevent fights by keeping it out in the open, but that probably stopped few.

CARDS OF THE PERIOD

Playing cards have gone through a lot of changes over the years. By the 1600s, the "French" deck had become standard. It is pretty close to the cards we know today. It had fifty-two cards and had the same marks that are used today: hearts, clubs, diamonds, and spades. Older types of decks had lots of different suits: acorns, bells, falcons, ducks, cups, swords, etc. There were the standard court cards: king, queen, and jack. The main difference is that there were no small numbers (indices) in the corners. Also, the court cards (face cards) were not double-sided as is standard now. The cards were larger. Because of this, and the lack of indices, they were usually held in two hands. Jokers were not introduced until 1850.

GAMING SUPPLIES

Cards: You can play the card games with a modern deck of cards, but it's more fun to use the older style deck.

Dice: You can use regular dice or make some of your own. (See instructions on page 199.)

Coins: You might get some period coins for your bets. You can also use pennies, beans, or candy to bet with.

For places to order cards, dice, coins, and other period games, see the on Gaming Supplies listed on our website at www.noquartergiven.net/merchant.htm. Once you get your dice, cards, and coins, recruit a few fellow buccaneers, learn the rules for some of the games that follow, and have a rousing game with lots of betting, cheating, and arguing.

ONE-AND-THIRTY

This old game is an early version of blackjack, only instead of playing to 21, you try to get to 31, or as close as possible without going over.

RULES —

Number of players: 2 to 8

Equipment: Standard deck of 52 cards.

Object: To be the first player to reach 31 exactly, or to be the player who comes closest to 31 without going over.

Deal: Before starting, everyone puts one coin or bean into the pot. To see who will be dealer, you each pick a card. The lowest card is dealer. Going to the left, the dealer deals three cards face down, one card at a time, to each player.

Play: Starting with the person to the left of the dealer and ending with himself (going clockwise), the dealer asks whether they want to "stick" or "have it." If the player wishes to "stick," the dealer goes to the next person. If they will "have it," they get another card. They may continue to get more cards until they decide to stick, or until they go over 31, in which case they are out.

Scoring: Number cards are worth their number of points; court cards (King, Queen, Jack) are worth ten. The Ace is worth 1. (The Ace cannot be switched between 1 and 11 as in modern Blackjack.) If all players have gone out (that is, gone over 31) before the dealer gets to himself, he wins without having to take a turn.

First player to reach exactly 31 wins on the spot. Hitting 31 exactly is worth a double stake (you get an extra coin or bean from everyone).

If no one reaches 31 exactly and more than one player is left at the end, the player closest to 31 wins the pot, which is a single bet from each player. If there is a tie, the player who went first (the one closest to the dealer's when going around the circle clockwise) wins.

For the next round, the position of dealer rotates to the left (clockwise).

LIAR'S DICE

Some say the conquistador Pizarro learned this game of bluff and lying from the South American natives he conquered. They were the Incan people, who lived in the area now called Peru. Who knows how old the game was before that.

This game is still very popular in South America, usually called Perudo, or Dudo. Its popularity is similar to the popularity of Bingo in the United States. People gather in special parlors to play and bet on Perudo. It is also a popular game in the pubs and taverns of London. In the United States, it is usually called "Liar's Dice" or "I Doubt It."

There are many, many variations to this game with different rules on how to bid, how to challenge, and how to lose. You can even find online versions to play against other online players. Here, we will teach you our favorite version, very similar to the dicing game you see Will Turner play against Davy Jones in *Pirates of the Caribbean 2*.

RULES —

Number of players: Up to 6 players, as long as you have enough dice to go around (you can squeeze in more people, but it slows down the speed of play).

Equipment: 5 six-sided dice for each player; 1 shaker cup for each player (you can use plastic cups, but they need to be solid in color, not see-through); plenty of pennies or beans to bet with.

Object: To be the LAST player with any dice.

First Player: Everyone roles one die. The player with the highest roll goes first.

Play: Each player starts with five dice and a shaker cup. Everyone shakes their dice in the shaker cup and then turns the cup upside down on the table. Each player may peek into their cup but should be careful to keep the dice hidden so no one else sees them. The First Player begins bidding. He/she bids on how many total dice under all the cups are displaying a certain number of pips (dots). Example: If the First Player has two 4s, then they are fairly safe in saying "I bid three 4s." The likelihood someone else has another 4 is good, and that would make the bet good. For the purposes of bidding, a 1 (Ace) is wild and can count for any number 2 through 6.

Based on their own dice numbers, players make higher bids in turn. We will continue with the example of "three 4s." The next player may increase the number of the pips on the die (example: "I bid three 5s"), or the quantity of dice displaying that number (example: "I bid four 4s") or both (example: "I bid five 5s"). Neither number may go down.

Each player must either make a bid or challenge the previous bid. To make a challenge, you do not bid. Instead, you call the previous bidder a "liar" very loudly. Then everyone lifts their cups and show all the dice. If the bid was "six 5s," then count the total number of 5s showing. Remember to include the 1s (wild dice) in the count. If there are six or more 5s (plus wild dice) showing, the player wins. If there are less than six 5s showing, the challenger wins.

Whoever is the loser of the challenge takes away one of their dice. Also, if the bidder who was challenged is the loser, he/she pays the pot a number of coins equal to the difference between their last bid and the actual number of dice counted. (Example: The bid was six 5s, but there are only four 5s, so the bidder pays 2 coins to the pot.) If the challenger loses, EVERYONE except the last bidder (winner of the challenge) pays a coin to the pot.

The dice are shaken again for the next round. Bidding starts with the player who won the previous challenge.

The last player with any dice is the winner and wins the pot of coins.

Strategy Tips: Remember, this is a game where you can LIE. You can make a bid on a number even if you don't have ANY dice with that number. You need to bluff and make the other players believe that you are telling the truth.

You might be a little careful at first about challenging. It's better to watch the other players to get an idea of what kind of players they are and see how many times they bluff.

Cheating: Do you think a TRUE pirate would play honestly? The fun of cheating is to do it rather obviously, then see who is paying attention and calls you out for it. Then, as two pirates would, you can get into a loud argument and use some of your best insults against each other (see the Pirate Insult Kit on page 97 for help here).

Cap'n Michael says:

If the opponent yer playing against is bigger'n you, cheatin' may not be such a good idea. Remember you can only run so far on a ship!

ROLLING THE BONES

D ice have been found in Egyptian tombs and in many of the ancient cultures. They were used to make major and minor decisions ("The die is cast"). People believed the gods controlled the outcome. Rolling dice was a method to find out what the gods wanted people to do. "Lady Luck" was a goddess. Her name was Fortuna, the daughter of Jupiter. Many a gambler has prayed to her for luck.

Originally, dice were made out of bone or ivory. They often used the knucklebones from animals. Even today, tossing the dice is called "rolling the bones."

Dice were tossed straight out of the hands or from a special dice box. As a pirate, you might use your drinking mug as a shaker cup for playing dice games. With a few dice in his pouch, a pirate was always ready for a quick game with others.

Here are some ways to make your own pirate dice.

NICE DICE

You will need:

+ Oven bake clay or polymer clay (clay that will not dry out when exposed to air. To harden it, you bake it in your oven at a low temperature. The surface can be painted and decorated. It comes in many colors.)
+ Dinner knife or some other tool with a flat edge
+ Dull pencil or ballpoint pen
+ Permanent black marker
+ Sand paper (optional)

If you are making dice for Liars Dice, you might want to make dice in sets of five, with each set a different color of clay (you can mix two colors of clay to get a third color).

First, soften and warm up the clay by rolling it around in your hand for a few minutes. Roll the piece of clay into a long snake shape.

To make one set of five dice, use the dinner knife to cut off five equal-sized lumps of clay. If the lumps are not exactly the same size, that will be

ROLLING THE BONES

(Continued)

okay. Cover your unused clay with plastic wrap or put it in plastic bags to keep it clean.

Roll each lump into a ball shape. Don't worry if it is not a perfect ball. Hold the clay ball between your thumb and index finger and squeeze a little to flatten two sides. Rotate a little and flatten the next two sides. Rotate one more time and flatten the last two sides.

Use a pointed object like a dull pencil or ballpoint pen to make the holes for the pips (dots). Push it in about ⅛ inch deep for each dot. Remember, opposite numbers on a die should add up to seven. So the 1 and 6 should be opposites, 2 and 5 are opposites, and 3 and 4 are opposites.

When your dice are shaped right, put them on a cookie sheet covered in foil, or in a flat, glass baking dish. Follow the baking instructions on the clay package to bake the dice (roughly 15–20 minutes at 250 to 275 degrees).

Let the dice cool completely when done baking before you handle them. When cool, use a permanent marker to darken the inside of the hole of each of the pips.

Variation: On the face of the die with one pip, use the permanent marker to draw a skull and crossbones.

Test Your Dice: Your dice won't be perfectly balanced, but you can fix any that are too far out of balance. Roll each of your dice 100 times. Keep a tally of how many times each side comes up. Out of 100 times, each number should come up 14–18 times. If one number comes up a lot more than that, that die is probably out of balance and won't be fair for play. Using sandpaper, you can sand down the opposite side to the number that comes up most, to take away a little weight from it. Then roll another 100 times and see if the division of numbers is more evenly balanced.

Or if you want to cheat (as we are sure some pirates did), take note of which dice favor certain numbers and don't sand them down. You can even make some of these unbalanced dice on purpose.

NOT SO NICE DICE

At times, you might want to play a trick on your shipmates and have a little fun and a good laugh. See how long it is before your friends catch on. Here are some ways to make trick dice.

† Follow the instructions above, but when you are marking the dots, on one side, instead of putting the two numbers that add up to 7, repeat one of the numbers. (Example: Instead of marking opposite sides as 1 and 6, make the two sides 6 and 6.) Then the number that is repeated will show up twice as often when you roll that die. For Liar's Dice, don't make all five dice in the set this way. That would be too obvious. Just make one or two dice this way.

† When making your clay dice, push some round steel ball bearings into the clay on one side. That side will be heavier and tend to land more on that side. The opposite number to that side will then show more when the dice are rolled.

CHEESE DICE

The food aboard ships was often not very good. Cheese was one of the common provisions. The type of cheese they used started out hard, and after weeks and months at sea, it got harder and drier. Instead of eating it, some sailors carved buttons and dice out of it!

For fun, you could try carving some dice out of a chunk of Edam (best) or cheddar cheese you left out to dry for several days.

MUSKET BALL DICE

Colonial troops in the 1700s were not allowed to gamble or carry dice (it led to quarrels over cheating, the same reason why many pirate crews banned gambling aboard ship). The soldiers did carry extra musket balls stored in a leather shot pouch.

Resourceful soldiers made crude dice from round musket balls using a hammer. They carefully flattened the sides of the balls into a cube shape. They made the pips (dots) using a nail.

They kept their dice in the shot pouch with the other musket balls, out of sight from the sergeant. But when he wasn't looking, the dice could come out for a quick game.

Beware: Musket balls were made of lead, and lead is TOXIC (poisonous). If you want to try making your own musket ball dice, you must get musket balls that are made from nontoxic materials.

SHIP, CAPTAIN, AND CREW

Popular in taverns of port cities or aboard seagoing vessels, Ship, Captain, and Crew is one of the favorite dice games of sailors.

RULES —

Number of players: 2 or more players (3–6 is best)

Equipment: 5 six-sided dice; plenty of coins (or beans) to bet with.

Betting: Each player places a coin (or bean) in the pot.

Object: To get the highest score.

First player: Everyone rolls one die. The person with the highest number gets the first turn. The next turn goes to the person to their left.

Play: First, everyone makes their bet by placing the amount agreed upon in the pot. Players each take a turn throwing the dice. During each turn, the player gets five throws of the dice. They roll and try to put to one side a 6 (the ship), a 5 (the captain), and 4 (the first mate). The numbers must be placed aside in descending order. You must get the ship (6) first so you have someplace for the men. Then you can't have a crew without a captain, so you must get the 5 next. The crew must have a first mate, to bring them the captain's orders, so the 4 comes next. (Example: if the first throw contains a 6 and 4, but not a 5, only the 6 is put aside and the rest of the dice, including the 4, are rolled again.)

If a player fails to throw the 6, 5, and 4 after their five throws, then their ship sinks, and they get no score.

Once a player has a ship with a captain and first mate (6, 5, 4), then the remaining two dice are the crew. Add the numbers of the two remaining "crew" dice to get your score. If you have not used up all five rolls, you may choose to roll the "crew" again until you have made five rolls in trying for a higher score. However, even if the score is lower, you are stuck with the last roll. A 2 is the lowest possible score while 12 is the highest score.

Keep a total of each player's scores. The player with the highest score after 10 rounds (or less if this is too long) takes the pot. If there is a tie, the tied players go for a final play-off round.

MAKIN' YER OWN
SWEAT-CLOTH GAME

You will need:

† 1 piece of plain cotton cloth (no printed designs),
   at least 24 x 24 inches (bigger is better)
† 1 piece of colored chalk
† Ruler or straightedge
† Wide permanent marker (black or red is best)
† Sewing pins
† Needle
† Thread (can match cloth or be a contrasting color)

The cloth you use for your "board" should be plain, without any designs. You need a blank "canvas" to start with.

Use the chalk with your straightedge to make a rectangle about 21 inches wide by 14 inches high. Divide the two 21-inch lines into three approximately equal sections of about 7 inches each (you can eyeball it or use the ruler) with little "tic" marks. On the two 14-inch lines, draw a tic mark to divide the line into two equal segments. Now, connect these points with the same point on the opposite line. You should end up with six boxes, about 7 x 7 inches each. There will be three boxes in the upper box and three boxes in the lower row. (See the illustration on page 205.) Once you have your lines measured and laid out in chalk, go over them with the permanent marker.

Starting with the left box of the upper row, with your marker, draw a large dot in the middle of the box (about the size of a penny). In the second box in the row, draw two dots, near opposite corners. In the third box, draw three dots in a row diagonally. The first box of the bottom row gets four dots (one near each corner). Five dots are placed in the middle box of the bottom row (four corners plus one in the middle). Six dots (two rows of three) are drawn in the last box.

To keep the edges of the cloth from unraveling, hem up the edges. Fold one edge of the cloth under by ¼ inch. Then fold it under again and pin it in place.

MAKIN' YER OWN SWEAT-CLOTH GAME

(Continued)

Do this for all four edges of the cloth.

With a length of knotted thread on your needle, start at one end of the corner under cloth; make stitches about ¼ inch apart, up and down, until you reach the other corner. Then turn the corner and continue making stitches until you go around all four sides of the rectangle. Tie off the thread and you are done. Sailors (and pirates) knew how to sew very well, so make the stitches as neat and as even as you can.

Now you are ready to wear your sweat-cloth. Fold your cloth in half diagonally, taking one corner and bringing it across to the opposite. This will form a triangle. Roll up the longest side a little, and then wrap it around your neck. Keep a couple of dice in your pocket. Then, when the bos'un or the mate aren't looking, or when your friends come over, you can whip off your game board and play a few rounds of sweat-cloth.

A GAME YOU KEEP AROUND YOUR NECK

This is a game of three dice and lady luck.

RULES—

Number of players: 2 or more

Equipment: 3 six-sided dice; a playing area marked with six squares (three on top, three on bottom), each marked like one of the 1–6 faces of a dice cube; coins (or beans) to bet with.

Object: To get the most winnings!

Dealer: Each person rolls one die. The player with the highest number will be the first dealer.

Betting: Players place their bets on the squares marked with 1–6 dots. More than one person can put a bet on the same number.

Play: The dealer rolls all three dice.

Players are paid as follows:

If a player's number comes up on one die, they are paid the amount of their bet.

If a player's number comes up on two dice, they are paid twice the amount of their bet.

If a player's number comes up on all three dice, the lucky dog is paid three times what he bet.

The dealer claims all losin' bets.

For the next round, the position of dealer rotates to the next player to the left (clockwise). Then the players bet again, and so on.

NOTE: Sweat Cloth is also known as "Crown and Anchor." For this version of the game, it is played with special dice. Instead of 1–6 dots, they have the four suits found in cards (hearts, clubs, spades, diamonds), plus a black anchor and a red crown.

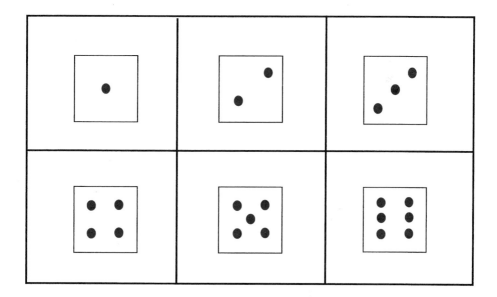

This game got its name because sailors used to draw or paint the playing area on their bandannas. They could get up a quick game when the mate wasn't looking. Then when the mate came near, they could quickly wrap up the "board" around their neck and pocket the dice with no one the wiser. Talk about bein' sneaky!

'ELLO, BEASTIE

MERMAIDS: LADIES OF THE SEAS

 ye, there's been many a sailor who's claimed to have seen a mermaid sitting on the rocks or heard her lovely singing off in the distance. Beautiful as they are, they are not something any sensible sailor would want to fool with. Read on, and we'll tell you why in these tales of the mermaid . . .

Mermaids are one of the oldest myths of humanity. The first tales about mermaids came from ancient Greek myths. The Greek poet Homer wrote about sirens in his epic tale *The Odyssey*. He made no mention of them being half fish, but it is believed his sirens were actually mermaids. The sirens in this great story sat on rocks, singing beautiful mesmerizing songs that lured men to their deaths.

Mermaids represent the beauty, mystery, danger, and romance of the seas. Almost every seafaring culture has developed mermaid tales. There are many, many variations in the mermaid folklore, but almost all of them describe the mermaid in the same way. She is a beautiful young girl, naked from the waist up, with long blond or green hair, very pale skin, and blue or sea green eyes, and her bottom half is that of a fish, complete with a fin and a spreading tail.

Romance and love were the basis of many of the legends. Mermaids were attracted to handsome men and wanted them for their husbands. In some of the tales, they preferred human men because mermen were not handsome. They were ugly, gross creatures with green teeth. In other tales, mermaids had no souls but could get one by marrying a man.

To have a human as a husband, she would have to lure him into the sea, where he would either join her in her undersea home or drown. In the tales, sailors heard these beautiful, haunting melodies drifting across the waves and sailed toward the wonderful music. As they sailed closer, they saw a mermaid sitting on rocks by the edge of the sea. She was playing a lyre and singing. Entranced by her songs, they sailed closer and closer until they crashed on the rocks. Sometimes, the sudden appearance of the ship startled the mermaid and she dove beneath the waves and disappeared. Thus, the sailors escaped their doom.

Mermaids captured landsmen in the same way. They would sit on rocks, just offshore. When the unlucky landsman came by, he was hypnotized by the mermaid's music and walked right out into the sea.

The tales say mermaids are very vain. They love to brush their long hair and look at themselves in a mirror. Many stories say they are holding a brush or comb and a mirror. These items often had magical powers, and if you stole one of them, you would have power over the mermaid.

It wasn't just mermaids who were attracted to men. Sometimes men were attracted to mermaids. If a man wanted to marry a mermaid but didn't want to live with her beneath the sea, then he had to capture her. If he succeeded, she would agree to stay on shore and become his wife, but only if she was allowed to return at certain times to the sea. In other tales, a mermaid would be kept as a wife only if he managed to steal one of her magical possessions such as her comb, brush, or mirror, and keep it hidden from her. He would need to hide it well, because no matter how long they were married, if she ever found it, the mermaid always returned to the sea, leaving a grieving husband and children behind.

Encounters between men and mermaids could be extremely dangerous. If a mermaid was attracted to a sailor and he rejected her, she could call up a storm or tidal wave to destroy the man who scorned her. Or she could lure his ship and cause it to crash on the rocks. If you were unkind to a mermaid, tried to take advantage of her, or, even worse, tried to harm her, her wrath could be terrible. Mermaids were said to have the power to call up storms, floods, and even tidal waves. A mermaid's vengeance could include not only you but your entire family as well! Her vengeance could even extend to your entire village or town. Sometimes whole coasts were destroyed after a mermaid had been insulted or misused.

On the other hand, being kind to a mermaid could be very rewarding. They had powers that could help seamen or destroy them. If a mermaid liked you, she might warn you of coming storms, lead you to a good place to find fish, or even save you from drowning. Being kind to a mermaid would bring good things, even good fortune. One legend has it that boats built by a particular boat builder would never sink because in the past one of the boat builder's relatives was kind to a mermaid and she granted his wish that none of the boats built by him or any of his descendants would ever sink.

Cap'n Michael says:

"What a wondrous thing that would be! Unsinkable boats backed by a mermaid's seal of approval! I think it's time that Cap'n Michael made friends with a mermaid!"

There are many superstitions about mermaids. If a mermaid were seen while the ship was at sea, it usually meant that the ship and its crew were doomed to sink. However, if the mermaid showed no interest in the ship or swam away, this would be a good sign.

Sailors knew meetings with mermaids could be very risky. If she approached the vessel because she was interested in someone aboard, and then he scorned her, she could call up a storm or tidal wave to destroy the entire vessel. Sailors believed if they threw fish or coins to the mermaid, she would dive for them and disappear, thus saving the ship from disaster. But the sailor or sailors who distracted the mermaid in this way might be in even more danger on the next voyage. If throwing fish or coins didn't work and the mermaid followed the ship, the ship was sure to sink.

Throughout the ages, it seems people wanted mermaids to be real. Numerous sightings of them and the multitude of stories written about these "ladies of the sea" show this to be true. There are stories of them in poems and books all around the world. They are portrayed in all kinds of art, from sculptures, paintings, vases, and other pottery works, to the figureheads on ships. Lamps, medallions, needlework, combs, and even chandeliers have been made with a mermaid motif.

Most of the written stories are about love and mermaids, or of mermaids who want to become human. Some stories are about mermaids having no immortal soul and how they try to obtain one by marrying a human.

Of the many stories written about mermaids, one of the most famous is *The Little Mermaid* by Hans Christian Andersen in 1836. When the mermaid turns fifteen, she falls in love with a handsome human prince. She seeks a magic spell from a witch that will give her legs. The mermaid pays a high price for this spell because although she is given the legs, every step she takes on land comes with a stabbing pain as if she were walking on a bed of sharp knives. In addition, the witch cut out the mermaid's tongue. As a result, the mermaid lost her voice. The mermaid endured all of this in order to be able to be with the prince she loved, but she didn't get what she wanted. The human prince jilted her to marry a human princess. The mermaid could have murdered the prince's bride, but instead she chose to die by throwing herself into the sea. By doing this, she earned an immortal soul with her sacrifice.

The 1913 bronze statue of Anderson's mermaid by Edvard Eriksen has become a national symbol in Denmark. The statue sits on a rock in the harbor at Copenhagen. The poor lass has been a target for vandals. Someone cut off her head in 1964. The crime was an unsolved mystery until thirty-three years later when Jørgen Nash, a writer, confessed that he cut off her head and tossed it into a nearby lake as a protest against society. Fortunately, the mold for making the original statue could be used to remake the missing part. Unfortunately, the original decapitation spawned copycats. Over the years, others have beheaded her, as well as cutting off her arms. She has also been painted a number of times by Danish taggers.

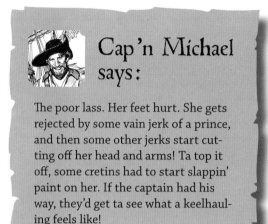

Cap'n Michael says:

The poor lass. Her feet hurt. She gets rejected by some vain jerk of a prince, and then some other jerks start cutting off her head and arms! Ta top it off, some cretins had to start slappin' paint on her. If the captain had his way, they'd get ta see what a keelhauling feels like!

Throughout the ages, there have been thousands of sightings of mermaids, some by famous explorers. Christopher Columbus reported he saw three mermaids in the Caribbean off Haiti. In 1608, the explorer Henry Hudson wrote the following in his logbook:

This morning one of our companie looking over board saw a Mermaid . . . from the Navill upward, her backe and breasts were like a woman's, her body as big as one of us; her skin very white; and long haire hanging down behinde, of color blacke; in her going downe they saw her tayle, which was like the tayle of a porpoisse and speckled like a Macrell.

Shakespeare wrote of mermaids in several of his plays. Mermaid signs were common in London at the time, indicating the building was a tavern. The famous Mermaid Tavern was where William Shakespeare and his contemporaries met.

British colonists brought their folklore and legends of mermaids to America. Harriet Beecher Stowe used this wealth of folklore in writing a story about a Maine sea captain who claimed he had spoken to a merman. In the story, the merman came to the surface of the sea and asked the captain to move the anchor of the boat. The merman explained that the anchor was blocking the door to his underwater home. His wife and children were trapped inside the home because of the anchor. Traditional sea chanteys have included the story. A verse of one such chantey goes as follows:

Oh, you've dropped your anchor before my house
And blocked up my only door,
And my wife can't get out, to roam about
Nor my chicks who number four.

People want to believe in mermaids and keep the romance going. Sometimes people are very gullible. They have fallen for many hoaxes that mermaids have really been found and are alive, or that there is proof of their existence. The most famous hoax was by P. T. Barnum (of the famous circus duo of Barnum and Bailey). Barnum had an exhibit that he claimed was the remains of a real mermaid found in the Fiji Islands in the South Pacific. What was actually exhibited was made by a Japanese taxidermist using parts from a monkey and a fish.

Barnum sent engravings of these remains of a "real mermaid" to newspapers. He distributed 10,000 posters and pamphlets with drawings depicting what this real mermaid supposedly had looked like when alive. It was exhibited in Barnum's American Museum in New York in 1842. The exhibit drew thousands of people to the museum. Barnum had several letters of scientific authentication—written by himself—and a friend of Barnum posed as a professor who declared it the mummy of a real mermaid. Finally, in 1855 Barnum confessed to the fraud. The funny thing is that, even with the confession, people still thronged to see the "FeeJee mummy" when it was taken on traveling road shows. After it arrived back in the American Museum, there were always long lines of people wanting to get a glimpse.

There have been thousands of sightings of mermaids, so there must be something to the stories. What is out there that causes people to think they have seen a mermaid? It has been suggested that dugongs or sea lions are what people actually see. These are large aquatic sea animals. They rise up out of the water and, in the fog, a sailor might mistake them for being part human. Manatees could take the blame for the vision of a mermaid with long hair. Just imagine a manatee coming up to the surface through a patch of seaweed. The seaweed could give the impression of long hair.

People do want to believe in mermaids. Look at all the books, movies, games, and dolls out there. Who knows, maybe there are mermaids out there somewhere. Maybe the sailors have it right after all.

LET'S GET KRAKEN

Have you ever been out in a boat on the ocean? Ever wonder what was in the water beneath you, just out of sight? Ever worry there was some monster hidden in the deep beneath your boat, about to leap up and gulp you down its gigantic mouth? Just about everyone who's been out to sea has thought the same thing.

There are many tales and legends to explain unexplainable things about the sea. There are a multitude of stories about sea monsters, mermaids, ghost ships, sprites,

The Kraken

by Alfred Lord Tennyson

Below the thunders of the upper deep;
Far, far beneath in the abysmal sea,
His ancient, dreamless, uninvaded sleep
The Kraken sleepeth: faintest sunlights flee
About his shadowy sides: above him swell
Huge sponges of millennial growth and height;
And far away into the sickly light,
From many a wondrous grot and secret cell
Unnumber'd and enormous polypi
Winnow with giant arms the slumbering green.
There hath he lain for ages and will lie
Battening upon huge sea-worms in his sleep,
Until the latter fire shall heat the deep;
Then once by man and angels to be seen,
In roaring he shall rise and on the surface die.

and Davy Jones and his locker. These and similar tales are found in cultures around the world. Different cultures prayed to various gods as well as making offerings and sacrifices in the belief that the gods had power to make things better if they were pleased. It was also believed that if the gods were not pleased, they had the power to do awful things. Now, the gods were thought to be good as long as they were happy, but there were also evil creatures that wanted to harm mankind and destroy it. One such monster was the legendary kraken.

Sailors from all over the world told the same stories—tales of seeing tentacles like that of a squid or octopus sticking out of the ocean. Only these tentacles were much, much larger. There were tales of seeing huge round heads with green eyes the size of dinner plates staring up through the water.

These sailors said they knew the answer to why so many vessels had just vanished without a trace. There was a monster prowling the depths of the sea—and it liked to drag ships down to their doom. It was the kraken!

Besides ships disappearing, there were also reports of WHOLE ISLANDS disappearing. One minute an island was there, and the next it was gone!

Even though no one had seen one of these monsters attack (and survived to tell of it), there were many tales of the monster's huge tentacles wrapping around a ship and dragging the crushed remains to the bottom of the sea. Some sailors said the monster was able to create a huge whirlpool under a ship, causing the vessel to sink. Other sailors said this creature could burst out of the ocean, leaving a hole in the water. The hole would then turn into a whirlpool that sank the ship. Most people figured those sailors had just been drinking too much!

The word "kraken" comes from Scandinavian tales of sea monsters. The creatures were said to dwell in the frigid waters off the coasts of Norway and Iceland. But stories of similar beasts came from all over.

There were newspaper accounts of sightings of these sea monsters. Famous poets and authors used these reports of sea monsters, disappearing ships, and vanished islands in their stories and poems. In 1830, Alfred Lord Tennyson wrote his famous poem "The Kraken." Jules Verne wrote *Twenty Thousand Leagues Under the Sea* in 1870. He did not refer to his sea monster as a kraken, instead calling it a giant squid, but it fit the same description. All of this strengthened many people's beliefs that this monster was real.

Sea monsters became all the rage in the 1800s. Jules Verne wrote: "They sang of it [the sea monster] in the cafes, ridiculed it in the papers, and represented it on the stage. All kinds of stories were circulated regarding it."

More recently, these monsters have been in a number of films, including *Walt Disney's 20,000 Leagues Under the Sea* and *Clash of the Titans*. In the *Pirates of the Caribbean* series, the kraken didn't attack ships and sailors for himself. It did the dirty work for Davy Jones by bringing sailors and ships to Davy Jones' locker at the bottom of the sea.

From watching these movies or reading stories with krakens and other scary sea monsters, you might have a nightmare or two. But, of course, you realize this is just an imaginary monster. So you can go boating or swimming in the ocean and not worry about a big monster coming out of the waters and grabbing you or your boat with its long undulating tentacles.

If you thought that, you would be WRONG!

Remember, there were thousands of reports by many credible people reporting they actually saw gigantic squids or parts of the animal showing above the ocean waters.

But don't feel bad if you thought that way. You weren't the only one. For a long time, scientists who should have accepted these reports denied there was such an animal. As none of the scientists had seen one nor did they have any photographs of them, they thought giant squid were just a myth.

Part of the problem was that these animals were seldom seen. They usually stayed at the bottom of the deep parts of the oceans where the waters were colder. Scientists had not yet developed the tools needed to explore the ocean depths.

Then in 1861, the sailors on the French steamer *Alecton*, cruising somewhere near the Canary Islands in the eastern Atlantic, saw something strange in the water. They fired a cannon and muskets at it, and then they gave chase. When they got close to this large thing, they threw harpoons at it, but the harpoons would not stick in the flesh. Then they managed to get a noose around it. When they started pulling on the rope, the rope sliced through the monster's flesh, cutting it to pieces. The monster then sank into the sea. The captain did manage to get a piece of the tail and decided what they had seen was a gigantic squid. The tail was taken to the French Academy of Science. The scientists there said the tail was not part of a giant squid because no such animal could be real. It was against the laws of nature. Despite the evidence right in front of them, the educated scientists said the monster did not exist.

Then in 1878, fishermen at Timble Tickle Bay, Newfoundland, saw a huge mass floating in the water. They saw that it was a giant squid—and it was still alive. They pulled it to the edge of the beach and tied it to a tree. When the tide went out the giant squid died. They measured it; the body part was 20 feet long and the longest tentacle was 35 feet, making this giant squid 55 feet in length. The suckers on the tentacles were four inches across. Unfortunately, they didn't take any of it to show the scientists. They just chopped the monster up for dog food! Imagine the commercials! A new taste sensation for pooches—Squid-Flavored Dog Food!

In 1930, the *Brunswick*, a Royal Norwegian Navy tanker, reported it was attacked three times by a giant squid. The squid tried to wrap its tentacles around the hull of the ship, but it couldn't get a good grip. It slid off and fell into the ship's rudders. More chopped squid for dog food!

On its maiden voyage, the sonar system of a U.S. Navy nuclear submarine failed. The sub returned to port for repairs. On examination, they found a rubber-like cover of the sonar system had been torn off. Embedded in the remains of the rubber were squid-like hooks. The size of the hooks indicated a very large squid had attacked them.

Perhaps the sub and the tanker looked like whales to the squid. Giant squids and whales are enemies and attack each other. In 1966 in South Africa, a giant squid was

An imaginary sea monster so large a ship can rest on its back while the crew celebrates Mass.

observed fighting a baby whale. The squid eventually killed the whale.

In 1965, a Russian whaler observed a giant squid attacking a 40-ton whale. Both animals died.

Many full-grown sperm whales have been seen with scars from the suckers of giant squid, which gives you an idea of their size and ferocity.

In the last half-century, there have been many, many documented reports of giant squid. There was one report in the 1980s of a giant squid just north of San Francisco.

What about reports that the monster shot up out of the water leaving a big hole that turned into a whirlpool? That couldn't have happened, could it? Well, perhaps it might have. Squid and octopuses can squirt water out of their body in a jet stream. The push of the squirting water quickly moves the squid or octopus along. Perhaps if the water is squirted downward, the force of the jet might shoot the animal straight up out of the water. When he fell back into the water, the whirlpool would be a natural result as he pulled the water down with him. It wouldn't last very long, but it would be a whirlpool.

Now what is the connection between the giant squid and disappearing islands? The answer is simple. On the rare occasions when a giant squid comes to the surface, it has been observed to stretch its tentacles straight out along the surface of the water. If you saw one from a distance, you might mistake it for a small island.

Scientists finally agreed there is such an animal as a giant squid. In 1905, two naturalists on a scientific cruise spotted such an animal off the coast of Brazil. It is agreed that other observations of squid up to 80 feet long are valid, but we don't know how much bigger a giant squid can get. There could be much bigger ones out there, waiting in the deep.

The giant squid is the largest invertebrate (animal without a backbone) on the planet—that we know about. Scientists still have a LOT to learn about these creatures. They know more about extinct dinosaurs than they know about giant squids.

Even though we know there are giant squids in the ocean, we also know they do not like warm water. They are seldom seen because they usually stay at the bottom of the ocean—but not always!

There has been no actual proof a giant squid has ever eaten a man or sunk a ship, though they have been seen attacking whales, ships, and submarines.

Here's something to think about: If a giant squid sank a ship, everyone on board would be missing and dead. So how would anyone really know what happened?

Just a bunch of sailors' old superstitions you say? Maybe so. But if you're sailing along and all of a sudden you see a big green eye more than a foot across, looking at you, you might want to sail faster!

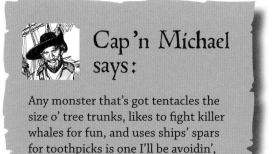

Cap'n Michael says:

Any monster that's got tentacles the size o' tree trunks, likes to fight killer whales for fun, and uses ships' spars for toothpicks is one I'll be avoidin', let me tell ya.

I'VE A HANKERIN' FOR GOLD!

ARE PIRATES LONG GONE? THINK AGAIN!

Recent news articles have headlines like "Cruise ship passengers describe 'pop, pop, pop' of gunfire as pirates attacked" and "$3M Ransom Parachuted to Tanker Pirates." The pirates have returned! True, certain things have changed. They have traded in their cutlasses for AK-47s, their sloops for speedboats, their cannons for rocket-propelled grenades, and their compasses for handheld GPS devices. But they still go by the "take what you can, give nothing back" way of doing things.

Piracy has never completely disappeared. It probably never will. It comes and goes in waves. When there are strong navies on patrol, good economies, and plenty of honest work for sailors, there are usually few pirate attacks. But when times turn hard and there is a chance for easy money, pirates return.

Small yachts and sailboats have been attacked in various parts of the world throughout history, and these attacks have continued to modern times. If the victims are lucky, they are just robbed of their valuables. If they are unlucky, they might also lose their boat and maybe their lives.

Modern pirates also go after huge cargo ships and oil tankers. These ships often have just a handful of crewmembers, so it's not too hard to overcome them. Large ships and their crews have been held for huge ransoms. Sometimes these large ships just disappear—perhaps into pirate-friendly ports. There they are repainted, modified, and given new registry numbers.

People debate whether honest crews should carry weapons to fight against boarders. Some claim if weapons are present, attackers will get hold of them and use them against the crew. There are many nonviolent ways to repel attacks. Cargo ships and cruise liners often use strong blasts of water from fire hoses, ear-splitting barrages of sounds, electric fences, and motion-activated spotlights.

Many of the current pirates are land-based. They often have crooked local officials giving them support or at least ignoring what they are doing. Organized crime gangs are often involved.

As in times past, areas with complex coastlines, shallow deltas, swampy shorelines, and/or lots of small islands are places where it is easy for pirates to lie in wait and disappear again.

Piracy Reporting Centre:

The International Chamber of Commerce keeps records of modern pirate attacks. At their Commercial Crime Services website, you can view a Live Piracy Map (which shows all pirate reports for the current year), find archived maps for recent years, and read posted reports at their Piracy Reporting Centre. For more go to http://www.icc-ccs.org/

In the 1990s, pirates were out of control in the Strait of Malacca. For quite a few years, authorities could not put a stop to them. Then the local governments got organized and worked together to outsmart the pirates. Since then, piracy has greatly declined in the Strait of Malacca. But just as the flames of one hotspot are put out, another hotspot flares up.

The current hotbed of piracy is in waters off the coast of Somalia. With no central government and severe poverty, conditions in Somalia have been ripe for pirates to thrive. The Gulf of Aden borders the north coast of Somalia. This entrance to the Suez Canal is nicknamed "Pirate Alley" due to the large amount of pirate activity. This is the same area where pirates Thomas Tew, Henry Every, and William Kidd made their famous captures in the late 1600s and early 1700s..

Like the Treasure Fleets of the Spanish Main, many ships going through the Gulf of Aden are traveling in small fleets with armed escorts.

Other current piracy hotspots include Indonesia, Malaysia, Bangladesh, the Philippines, the Indian Ocean, West African coasts along the Gulf of Guinea, and Tanzania.

Piracy is still common in the South China Sea, where many of today's pirates are descendants of the famous Chinese pirates Koxinga and Cheng I, who were active from the 1600s to the 1800s.

Cap'n Michael says:

In this modern world, it's nice to know that good, old-fashioned family businesses are still going strong.

IMAGE CREDITS

Becker, Richard, original art by: 21, 49, 53, 161, 174, 186, [modified] 207

Dover Publications, Inc.: (pub. 2003) 29, 152, 193, 215; (pub. 1970) 176, 177, 180, 197

Gibbs Smith, Publisher: [scroll*] 5, [sea] 11–24, [flag: movie camera icon*] 34, [scroll/footsteps*] 94, [flag: chef's hat icon*] 164

Lampe, Christine Markel ** (Jamaica Rose),** original art by: [skull icon*] 4 (right), [corner art*] 8, 9 (upper left), 17, 26, 38, [small scroll*] 50, 58, [name scroll*] 63, 70 (lower), 77 (lower), 78, 79, 80 (upper 3 images), 81, 82–83, 84–85, [large scroll*] 98, [skull/notes*] 111, 124, 127–28, [medium scroll*] 171, 183, [3 skulls] 189; [private collection of] 5, 13 (upper), 22, 33, 136, 168, 169

Lampe, Michael ** (Captain Michael MacLeod):** [skull/crossbones*] 3, 9 (lower left), 80 (lower), [photos by] 84–85, [photo modified by] 86

Library of Congress, courtesy of: [sloop] 2, 12, 20 (lower right), 24, 57, 92, 155, 157, 158, 173

Library of Congress, Prints and Photographs Division, courtesy of: 154

Maitz, Don: [illustration] 9, [cropped illustration*] 11

No Quarter Given, courtesy of: 19, 64, 67, 77 (upper), 108, 124, 138–40, 142–44, 146, 195, 205

Public Domain: [cannon] 2 (2 images), 4 (left), 5, 12, 13 (2 images), 16 (right), 20, 22, 24, 32, 33, 40, 42, 57, 63, 65, 66, 92, 134, 136, 153, 154, 155, 156, 157 (2 images), 158 (2 images), 168, 169, 173, 196, 202

Reyes, Gerard, original art by, 68, 69, 70 (upper)

Whittam, Arthur, photograph by: [modified by Michael Lampe] 86

For further information on images in public domain and courtesy of the Library of Congress, please contact the authors.

* scattered throughout book
** authors

SET SAIL!

INDEX